An Extraordinary
Journey

AN EXTRAORDINARY
JOURNEY

DORIS GALLIPPI

Library of Congress Control Number:		2015944615
ISBN:	Hardcover	978-1-5035-8027-5
	Softcover	978-1-5035-8028-2
	eBook	978-1-5035-8029-9

Print information available on the last page.

Rev. date: 10/23/2015

To order additional copies of this book, contact:
Xlibris
1-888-795-4274
www.Xlibris.com
Orders@Xlibris.com
709434

CONTENTS

INTRODUCTION

The Family Immigration Road Map

This is the story of my family's first steps in America, the voyage they took to get here, the times in which they lived and the place they came to call home. Those dreams of opportunities that brought my grandparents to America catapulted family members from our old ethnic neighborhood to the far reaches of the United States in pursuit of success. Research on our family's history made clear our grandparents were far more adventuresome than my generation in pursuit of their success. With one exception, the older generation is gone from our time. Left in their wake are dozens of freshly minted Americans. As we reach to fulfill our dreams, the first voyagers' dreams for us are being fulfilled.

I am Doris Gallippi. My mother Catherine Marie Gaetano, now 101-years-old, was born in Italy and my father Anthony James Gallippi was born in America of parents who recently emigrated from Italy. Each of my parents was raised in an ethnic household within the same Larimer Avenue neighborhood of East Liberty, Pittsburgh, PA., just blocks from one another. Each of their parents made the journey to America separately. While the destination was the same, their individual experiences were different.

From the time the first grandparent journeyed to America in 1895 to the last who made the journey in 1922, America and Italy were on journeys of their own. Their stories are intertwined with America's story.

Those four voyagers forged the path for our family. Their decisions and sacrifices set the stage for our lives. They were the pioneers, the risk-takers, the reasons for the colorful nature of our family. They were the opportunity seekers and most importantly they were the dream seekers. The family mantra was "This is America... you can be anything you want to be if you work for it". The choices were ours as long as the kind of choices made were the kind of choices upon which successes could be built.

Meet the voyagers and travel with me through those times on this *"Extraordinary Journey."*

THE VOYAGERS

(Antonio at age 22)

Antonio Gaetano, father of my mother Catherine, journeyed to America in the winter of 1895 on the steamship *"SS Patria"*. He was a 15-year-old "Sojourner".

(Rosa at age 33)

Rosa Gaetano, mother of my mother Catherine, journeyed to America in 1922 at 33-years-old, 14 years after she married Antonio. She traveled on the steamship *"SS Colombo"* with 13-year-old Bruno; 8-year-old Catherine Marie; 20-month-old Anthony and 9-month-old Maria.

(Giuseppe at age 35)

Giuseppe Gallippi, father of my father Anthony, arrived in America on April 10, 1903 in search of economic success. He journeyed to New York from San Paulo, Brazil on the steamship *"SS CapFrio"* after working in Brazil for three years. He was a 28-year-old man married to Maria Catarina Teti Gallippi.

(Catarina at age 32)

Maria Catarina Gallippi, mother of my father Anthony, journeyed to America on the steamship the *"SS Koningin Louise"* on March 6, 1906, at 25-years-old with their 6-year-old child Victoria.

The two families, the Gaetano's and the Gallippi's were bound by their ethnicity and the Larimer Avenue Village neighborhood. Their American experiences are different parts of the Italian/American emigration mosaic.

This history has been documented by what could be substantiated through official papers, numerous sources and family stories. Where true facts existed they were used and footnoted. Some information gathered for this account comes from family recollections.

Since the principals in the story, those four grandparents and all their children but one, Catherine Marie, are no longer alive to share their stories. Their experiences have been written from the perspective of walking in their footsteps through circumstances that existed in their days. It seemed to be the best way to tell their stories.

THE DEDICATION

This social history of my family is being written with a tear in my eye. I can only think of my mother Catherine Marie, who, in her 101st year, has forgotten the extraordinary journey she and our family made across a great ocean from one culture to another on the journey to become Americans.

This book is for her, as she can no longer speak of the history to her grandchildren and great grandchildren.

If the story is not told, those who follow this lineage will only know of their lives in America. The richness of their heritage and how they got to be Americans would be lost. I know if my father were alive to read this story, he would have been pleased it had been written for those who followed.

CHAPTER 1

VOYAGER ANTONIO GAETANO
(July 3, 1880 - July 4, 1930)

The Gaetano Family Story Up To 1906

Waves arched in distant waters under a cloud-covered November sky in 1895 as 15-year-old Antonio Gaetano made his way to America. He stood on the lower deck of the steamship *"SS Patria"* escaping the cramped confines of steerage for a few precious breaths of fresh, cool ocean air. He was in pursuit of his destiny... to place his footprint on American soil. Antonio was an orphan. He was the 7th child in a family of 8 children born in the small town of Nicastro in the Province of Reggio de Calabria, Italy. His father and mother had both died before he reached his teenage years, and he had been beckoned to America to live with his father's brother Domenico and his wife Maria who had settled in America two years before.[1] In the middle of his 14-day voyage across the Atlantic he had plenty of time to feel the excitement of his new venture and to reflect on the Italy of his childhood.

Nicastro The Beautiful
Nicastro was the only home Antonio had known. Nicastro, as part of Calabria, is nestled in the arch of the foot of boot-shaped Italy, bordered to the north by the region of Basilicata; to the south-west by the region of Sicily, the Straight of Messina and the Mediterranean Sea; to the west by the Tyrrhenian Sea and to the east by the Ionian Sea.[2]

Four mountain ranges mark the Italian peninsula at that place. The Aspromonte, Pollino, Sila and Serra mountains with some of the highest peaks in Italy, and with landscapes that cascaded down to the sea coast towns below...towns like Nicastro. Lush, dense vegetation, clear water streams, lakes and beautiful waterfalls graced the mountains then, as they do today. Their towering peaks ranged from 6,500 feet to 7,500 feet. Antonio can remember as a young child going to the lower Pollino playing among the beech trees with his family, climbing on the dolomite-like rock formations, investigating the countless caves on that mountain and occasionally seeing a Royal Eagle flying overhead. He would hear of the Mercure Valley within the Pollino mountain range and the mysteries of its sanctuaries, convents and castles built by the original 14th & 15th Century Albanian settlers.

His fondest memory is of the time he and his father Bruno travelled to the ancient monastic complex of Serra San Bruno which St. Bruno of Cologne had established in 1090. St. Bruno was his father's patron saint and the grounds of the Carthusian Monastery provided an amazingly calm atmosphere. They contained the Santa Maria Del Bosco Church, the sepulcher of San Bruno and a small reflecting pond with a statue of St. Bruno kneeling on the spot where water sprouted up after the saint's bones had been dug up for placement in the Abby. The land in this area was rich-soiled agricultural land dotted with long established olive and fig trees. Other sections produced a variety of vegetables & herbs growing beside fruit orchards. Many of these items were exclusive to the coastal area within Reggio de Calabria. The climate and geologic conditions were perfect for the production of the most sought after 'essence oil' from the 'Bergamot Orange Olive' used in expensive perfume. The area was known for its world-renowned olives and cooking oils that had been cultivated since the 18th century.

There were the fish, of course, and 'fresh catch of the day' literally meant that. Fishermen would bring live fish back from a dawn excursion in the surrounding seas, sort and separate their catch by type, and place them in a waist-high, circular, partitioned stone tank in the town square. After the catch was in, local women would shop at the 'fountain', pick the fish of their choice and take it home wiggling in paper.

Highly prized Porcini mushrooms, that grew wild on the Serra mountain range above a nearby sea coast town, were gathered and prepared with olive oil and garlic as a side dish. In better times, a meal was either the fish of the day or chicken that came from home-raised stocks along with either home-made bread or fresh soup. Neither pasta made from semolina nor tomatoes had been introduced into the southern Italian diet at this time. Because Pietro Matthioli, an Italian

2

herbalist wrote in 1544 that the tomato was a poisonous plant,[3] It was believed tomatoes were poisonous well into the 1900's. Pasta dough at that time was made from corn meal.

For those of us who have eaten spaghetti with tomato sauce all of our lives, this seems ironic because more than half of contemporary southern Italian cooking in the United States and elsewhere is all about using tomatoes.

A History Note-Countryside Beautiful; but Impoverished

Belying the beauty of the region was the poverty of the people who lived in this highly stratified, feudal society. They were sharecroppers and farm laborers who eked out a meager existence and could only look forward to a dismal future. There was unemployment, under employment, high mortality, and little or no formal medical care. "Each day required long walks to family plots, adding to the toil that framed daily lives. For reasons of security and health, residents typically clustered in hill towns situated away from farm land."[4]

"Families worked as collective units to ensure survival."[5] Many felt this way of life "was continuous, inadequately rewarded labor."[6] A former, successful immigrant named Angelo Pellegrini said, "Education beyond the third grade was out of the question... at eight or nine years of age, if not sooner, the peasant child is old enough to bend his neck to the yoke and fix his eyes upon the soil in which he must grub for bread. I did not know it then, but I know it now; that is a cruel, man-made destiny from which there is yet no immediate hope of escape."[7]

Risorgimento Unifies Italy (1860-1870)

Before Antonio was born on July 3rd 1880, 19th Century Italy was in turmoil that spilled over into his generation. The 1860-1870 unification movement known as *'Risorgimento'* (resurrection) changed Italy's social and political face. The foundation for Italian unity was laid thirty years before in 1830 by Giuseppe Mazzini, a brilliant liberal nationalist.[8] His efforts came from the lingering results of a history filled with the Holy Roman Empire, Catholic Popes, Normans, Saracens and the Austrians, who all vied for control of various segments of Italy.

The Austrians, after the rebellion of 1848 and the battle of 1849, took over and marched into Rome to put Victor Emmanuel II, Italy's first king, in power.[9] The country had been fragmented for centuries. [10] Mazzini was one of the disappointed patriots who looked to the House of Savoy for leadership and to Count Camille di Cavour, the prime minister of Sardinia in 1852, to be the architect of a united Italy. After the Crimean War ended in 1856, Giuseppe Garibaldi conquered Sicily and Naples, and turned them over to Sardinia. Victor Emmanuel III, King of Sardinia, was then proclaimed king of Italy in 1861.[11] The Risorgimento process converted and unified the many different states existing within Italy at that time into one; and, is the configuration of modern-day Italy. There was strife... there was struggle... there was "a desire for independence" ... there was warfare in which most of the men who fought for freedom during this period were peasants seeking a chance for something better.[12]

"The newly unified nation of Italy faced nearly insurmountable problems. It had a very large debt, few natural resources, and almost no transportation or industry. This, combined with a high ratio of poverty, illiteracy and an uneven tax structure, weighed heavily on the people of the country in both the north and the south. Only a small fraction of Italians had voting rights.

Pope Pius IX (1846-1878) was angry because of the loss of the city of Rome and the Papal States, and refused to recognize the State of Italy."[13] Rome and central Italy, comprising states under the secular control of the Catholic papacy, formed a dividing line. To the south a secession of foreign monarchs ruled the kingdom of Naples and Sicily, exploiting the country-side without regard for the inhabitants. A feudal system persisted in which political power and social influence were based on hereditary possession of land. [14] If southern Italians hoped to improve their lot through unification, they were soon disappointed and found themselves worse off than before unification.

The northern-dominated government in Rome was ruthless, treating the south of Italy like a colonial possession by using the region to further increase industrial interests in the north through discriminatory government policies in trade, industry, and education. While peasant life in northern Italy improved dramatically with the introduction of crop rotation, machinery and fertilizers, few modern methods penetrated the south where large estates, owned by absentee landlords and supervised by overseers, were tilled by field workers with the same kinds of hand plows, hoes, and spades used for centuries.[15]

Epidemics of Cholera and Malaria spurred thousands of southern Italians into leaving the country. Along with disease came a mysterious parasite that destroyed most of the grapevines in southern Italy, the means through which many farmers made their living.[16] In the Italian rural areas, banditry and several other problems resulted in repression by the brutal government. During the 1880's a new movement started developing among the city workers. The huge differences between the impoverished, rural south of the country, where Antonio's family lived, and the wealthy, industrialized north increased.[17] Northern Italy, mostly under the direct influence of the Austrian House of Savoy, saw the emergence of industry and anchored it all in the north.[18] Italy was a nation in crisis. Even the efforts by a series of liberal politicians from 1870 to 1915 were not able to form a majority to facilitate needed change.[19]

The "Sojourners"

The mood of young men and older townsmen in Nicastro was dark. Daily there were talks of the powers of government and the ring of hopelessness. Antonio was among the young, an orphan with good looks, who was literate beyond other townsmen and ambitious. He felt there was no opportunity to make a living in southern Italy. There was no way to elevate himself.

Antonio, like other young southern Italian men looking for opportunity, joined an exodus from the peninsula. Some looked to Argentina and Brazil in South America as their destination. Others looked to the United States for refuge. The mass migration from southern Italy that started in 1871,[20] became a torrent of freeing humanity from 1876 through 1924 when more than 4.5 million Italians arrived in the United States.[21] Antonio's departure from Italy came in 1895 three years after America's Ellis Island opened its immigration port. Sojourners were looking for immediate employment, maximum savings, and quick repatriation.[22]

Many immigrants of the time felt they would be temporary Americans whose roots would remain in Italy. "The movement was

5

predominately composed of young, single men of prime working age, from 15 to 35 years old, who clustered in America's urban centers. Multiple trips were commonplace and ties to American society, such as learning English, securing citizenship and acquiring property, were minimal at the beginning of the movement. With eyes focused on the old-world *'Paese'* (village), at least half of the sojourners returned to Italy, although in some years rates were much higher. Such mobility earned Italians the 'birds of passage' label that persisted until women and families began to migrate and settlement became increasingly permanent in the years following 1910".[23]

Antonio's ideas were different from most Sojourners. He was an independent thinker, who even at the age of 15, had opened his mind to embracing America as his home. As his voyage neared its end, the beacon of prosperity shone brightly in Antonio's imagination, as bright as he imagined the Statue of Liberty would look in New York's harbor. He listened to stories about the statue from new friends on his voyage and the ship's crew, and how it had been built in France and would be in America this very year. After what seemed like an eternity, the *"SS Patria"* dropped anchor in New York Harbor just off Ellis Island on Thursday, November 28, 1895, on America's Thanksgiving Day. Although an older ship, formerly known as the *"SS Rugia"*, this was its first voyage from Naples to Manhattan as a newly named ship. On this crossing, the *"SS Patria"* carried 96 first class passengers; 1,100 passengers in steerage and 90 crew members as it made its way across the Atlantic at its maximum pace of 12 knots.[24]

Antonio scanned the water looking for the Statue of Liberty; but, saw no statue. Disappointed, he doubted all he had heard about America, and in his young mind, thought the stories had been a trick to get people to come to the U.S. to become slaves. He carried this fear until he was being processed some 12 hours later and was told, by his interpreter, the statue had arrived in New York on June 17th but could not be assembled because there was not enough money to build the 154 foot high pedestal upon which it was to stand. The interpreter told him there was one wealthy contributor but most of the $120,000 needed had been raised from the American people in small donations of less than a dollar.[25] He suggested Antonio look closely as he boarded the **'Railroad Ferry'** to the train that would take him inland, and he would see the beginnings of the pedestal.

From the Ship to Ellis Island

It was a cold November day as a ray of sun occasionally interrupted swirling snowflakes around the men cued up to exit the ship. In slow procession, clutching suitcases, with softer baggage held tightly under their arms, 1,100 men disembarked the ship. Cold hands clasped the ropes as they climbed down long fixed ladders to barge-like vessels below for the short jaunt to Ellis Island and solid ground. Each man would be given a name tag with his manifest number written in large figures. The men were assembled in groups of 30. According to the manifest of the **"SS Patria"** from that journey, Antonio was #627.

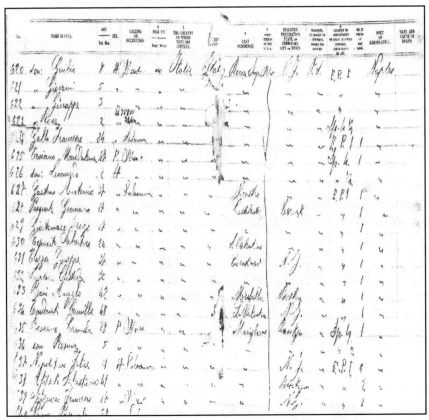

"SS Patria" Ship Manifest Showing Antonio's Name

He descended the ladder about half way in the procession. It was an orderly parade of exhausted men most of whom were wearing their best clothes but had not had the benefit of showers in steerage nor any way to wash their clothes for the $30 American each had paid for his passage. The rate included a guarantee of 60 cents worth of food per day. Passengers would tell you the meals were nutritious; but, not delicious. Most stories of steerage refer to the stench of arriving immigrants until they were given the opportunity on Ellis Island to shower, shave and dress themselves in clean clothes they had with them. Before showering, Antonio was met by his first American, a nameless interpreter who, with his patience and skill, helped Antonio understand what the next steps would be.[26]

After having been on the ocean for 14 days, Antonio could still feel the movement of the *"SS Patria"* under his feet in the **'Registry Room'** with the sounds of different languages spoken by immigrants from other countries as they were being processed. Interpreters led groups through the main doorway and directed them up a steep stairway to the doctors standing at the top of the stairs "watching for signs of lameness, heavy breathing or bewildered gazes that might be symptomatic of a mental condition".[27]

The doctor was called the *'Eye Man'* who looked for symptoms of Trachoma, an eye disease that caused blindness and death in some cases. This disease was the reason for more than half of the medical detentions and its discovery meant certain deportation. [28] It was well into the night before Antonio was blessed with that hot shower and passed his medical exam. Food to Antonio as he took his place in the **'Primary Line'.** He sat beside immigrants on one of a hundred long pipe benches waiting to be interviewed by an inspector. As morning arrived, Antonio was directed to sit on a metal chair, accompanied by with a different interpreter.[29] The chair was across from a high metal table. He was asked 29 questions and was required to show his passage papers; his passport papers; and, any money he had on his person. The money was counted by the inspector, noted and handed back to him. New immigrants were required to have enough money equal to $25 American before they were allowed to leave Ellis Island.

Antonio was asked to identify his sponsor, to explain where he was going and how he was going to get there. When he passed that test he was handed his **'Landing Cards'** and taken to the **'Money Exchange'** where he exchanged a few pieces of gold, some silver and Lire into American money based on the day's official rates posted on a blackboard.[30] Antonio's processing only took about 16 hours which was far less than for some who were suspected of various types of sickness. They were referred to the infirmary and remained on Ellis Island for a night or two if they were not sent back to their country of origin.

A History Note - Ellis Island

New York City was the main east coast immigration port of entry into the United States from the early 19th Century until the middle of the 20th Century. In the U.S., although immigration acts had been passed, there was no formal routine for implementing immigration policy on a national level until the federal government assumed direct jurisdiction in 1890. Previously the matter was delegated to the states via contract between the states and the federal government. At that time, most immigrants landing in New York would disembark at the docks along the Hudson and East Rivers in what is today Downtown Manhattan. On May 4, 1847 the New York State Legislature created the Board of Commissioners of Immigration to regulate immigration.[31]

When the federal government assumed control over immigration it established the Bureau of Immigration which chose the three-acre Ellis Island in Upper New York Harbor as a port of entry. The island, already a federal possession, had served as an ammunition depot. It was chosen due to its relative isolation as an island that was in close proximity to New York City and the rail lines in New Jersey, via a short ferry ride. The island needed improvements including expansion by land reclamation prior to it being used to receive immigrants so the federal government operated a temporary depot in a Barge Office at the Battery.[32]

Ellis Island opened on January 1, 1892, three years before Antonio arrived in America. It operated as a central immigration center until the National Origins Act was passed in 1924 which closed Ellis Island to emigrants. The island ceased all immigration processing on November 12, 1954.[33] Today, the Island is still owned by the federal government. It was added to the National Park System in May of 1965 by President Lyndon B. Johnson, and is part of the Statue of Liberty National Monument. Ellis Island was opened to the public as a museum of immigration in 1990.[34]

A History Note-America's People

Italians were, obviously, not the only immigrants to adopt America as their new home. There were those Pilgrim Voyagers who crossed the Atlantic Ocean on the *"Mayflower"*. For well over four centuries, people attempted to find refuge under this nation's protective wings as opportunists, sojourners, missionaries, refugees and illegal aliens.

With the Statue of Liberty greeting Europeans entering Ellis Island in 1896, and The Golden Gate Bridge greeting Chinese and other Asians in San Francisco, the U.S has long since been a refuge to peoples of the world, with opportunities abounding and freedom for all. Overtime millions have found emigrating to the U.S. as the only alternative to safety, starvation, death, or a life full of hardship and suffering. With thousands from nations spanning the globe, America has become a mosaic of people, culture, and hope.[35]

Antonio Completes Ellis Island Processing

Friday had finally arrived and Antonio walked through the last room toward the **'Railroad Ticket Office'.** He saw the face of his sponsor... Uncle Domenico. Accompanied by his wife Maria, Domenico had braved a fierce snow storm and arrived just hours before to meet Antonio in what was called the **'Kissing Room'** on Ellis Island, and take him to his new home.[35]

There was an embrace of relief, there were tears of expression at the completion of that long journey in steerage, and there was chattering and arm waiving all the way through another long line to board the **'Railroad Ferry'.**

Uncle Domenico knew a cold winter day in New York might be a difficult transition for his nephew who had spent his life in the temperate climate of a seacoast town in Italy. To give Antonio comfort, Domenico brought with him a winter coat he had borrowed from his cousin Luigi for this event. There is no record of how Luigi felt about this; and, we can only assume Antonio appreciated the gesture as he rode in the open-sided ferry boat across the frigid waters of the Hudson River.

The transport of immigrants was organized. Each had been given a clearly-marked ticket of transport before boarding the double-decker ferry. With his uncle and aunt, Antonio joined several hundred immigrants who had been cleared that day and traveled to the Central Railroad Station in Hoboken, N.J. Around midnight they boarded a steam-driven train to Philadelphia, the first leg of their 12-hour journey to Pittsburgh, PA.

Train Ride to the Future

Antonio sat on the straw-stuffed, bench-styled seat at the window. Vincenzo flipped the back of the next seat so he and Maria could face Antonio. Maria encouraged Domenico to sit beside his nephew to hear stories of relatives in Italy, or to talk about the politics of the time. Communication from the old country was limited and came only in letters written by literate men. Women were not allowed to learn to read or write so the letters would state family matters from a man's perspective. To understand the times it is important to note Antonio arrived in America about five years before another Italian named Guglielmo Marconi sent his first wireless communication from America to England.

It did not take long for Antonio to feel a pang of hunger. He had not eaten since he waited in line to be processed. Like most Italian women of the time, Maria's place was to meet the food needs of the family. She was prepared. She sensed his need, reached into the satchel tucked neatly beside her, and pulled out an apple for a surprised and grateful Antonio who was cradled in cousin Luigi's warm wool coat. Heat on the train was minimal, if at all. However, the homemade bread, hard sausage, several hard boiled eggs and a small jug of wine Maria had packed for the long train ride home promised a warming they would all soon welcome. Antonio smiled and chomped the apple as they rode. He had not had a fresh piece of fruit for over two weeks and craved the succulent pulp. Besides, by then, he knew he had not been tricked into coming to America, and would never be a slave. After a while, Maria, Domenico and Antonio took bites of bread and sausage to satisfy their hunger and sipped the wine. The eggs were reserved for the last hours of the trip. Antonio's need for rest overtook his excitement. He drifted in and out of sleep.

The first train took them about 50 miles from Philadelphia to a railway transfer station in Reading, PA. The dimly lit station known

12

as the 'Outer Station' sat in the middle of a sea of railroad tracks. There, in the night, they boarded a second train to Harrisburg, PA. At the Harrisburg Station, they transferred to a third train that would take them over the Tuscarora, Kittatinny, Allegheny and Summerset Mountains of Pennsylvania to Pittsburgh. It was well past noon on Saturday when the train pulled into the Pittsburgh station. The weather was nothing short of miserable with its low-hanging grey clouds. Black smoke from the steel mills clogged the air making it almost impossible to see. Streets were filled with people trudging through dirty snow that had fallen two days before and roof-tops had a curious look as heavy, soot-stained snow drooped at their edges. Through the bustle, teams of strong-backed horses pulling streetcars passed, their hot breath making clouds of their own as Uncle Domenico led the trio to the streetcar stop along Liberty Avenue. He hadn't thought about Antonio having no boots, only the soft-soled shoes he wore daily in Italy. Unlike his Aunt Maria, who tucked her head deep inside the hood of her wool cape, Antonio felt no cold in his excitement as he looked down the street waiting for the streetcar. Finally, the horses emerged from the grey and the streetcar stopped in front of them. The fare was paid by Domenico as they boarded.

There was no heat on the streetcars; but, the glass enclosure kept the elements out. In East Liberty, the trio transferred to another streetcar that would take them to Larimer Avenue. The six mile trip gave Antonio the opportunity to see new sites as a team of four snorting horses struggled to pull the streetcar through the slippery, snow-covered streets to Larimer Avenue.

A History Note- Pittsburgh & Transportation

By the time Antonio arrived from Italy, Italians had moved from their first settlement on Virgin Alley (later renamed Oliver Avenue in downtown Pittsburgh), to the Lower Hill District and then, as a colony, moved to the Larimer Avenue area. Pittsburgh's boundaries had been annexed through a campaign that tripled the size of the city south of the Monongahela River.[37] In 1870, fifteen years before Antonio's arrival, Pittsburgh's City Council passed the "Penn Avenue Act" that made paving local streets possible. As a result horse-drawn streetcar service was extended from downtown of Pittsburgh to East Liberty in 1872.[38] Antonio arrived in Pittsburgh on the cusp of this major, mechanical transportation change. Laying Bessemer steel rails became a significant source of jobs and income for immigrant laborers. Streetcars were still in their infancy. Steel rails that would carry passengers on streetcars in Pittsburgh and its developing surrounding communities had been installed in some places and only in the planning stages for others.

Larimer Avenue Village-An Italian Colony

The streetcar made about a half a dozen stops before it got to Larimer Avenue and the stop at Maxwell Way, a small side street off Larimer Avenue where Domenico and Maria lived. They rented the second floor of a 3-story house. Antonio remarked at the flatness of the village land, as it was unlike his mountainous surroundings in Nicastro. Domenico opened the front door and Maria entered the house, quickly climbing the stairs to their apartment. The smell of something cooking soon took Antonio's attention as did the warmth he had not felt in so many days. He sat on the steps in the vestibule to remove the shoes and socks from his wet feet when Mrs. Labriola, the lady living in the first floor apartment, opened her door holding a pot of warm chicken soup. She spoke softly to this shivering young man in rumpled clothing as she handed him the pot of soup. She knew full well how he felt. His was a journey she made with

14

her husband Franco, and their two young children Angelina and Benedetto, two years before. Antonio stood on his numbed feet. "Molte grazie", he said as he took the pot of soup and climbed the stairs. "This was going to be okay," he thought. "This was going to be okay."

The house had been converted from a single home to a three-unit apartment building. The four-room apartment, with its floral-patterned wallpaper and small wood-framed windows provided a homey welcome on the second floor. A full attic on the third floor was now housing for a third family. There were two doorways on the landing at the top of the stairs. One door opened to the attic apartment, and one opened to the second floor and a hallway that led to a large living room, bedroom, kitchen and a bathing room that would one day become a full bathroom. Plumbing in those days was limited to piping that brought water to the home through faucets in the kitchen, and bathing room that was outfitted with a sink and a cast iron bath tub. The water came from two large, city water reservoirs in the northern part of the neighborhood in an area that officially became known as Highland Park in 1889.[39] Sewer systems had not yet been installed in the annexed portion of Pittsburgh, so outhouses were perched in the back yards of these homes and chamber pots were used by residents. In some neighborhoods, outhouses were placed side to side in courtyards between two rows of attached houses.

The only source of heat in the apartment came from a large gas heater in one corner of the living room. A curtain had been hung at the back of the living room behind which a single bed and a shelf for Antonio's things had been placed. He didn't realize it at first, but, he would be sleeping in what was the warmest room of the apartment. When Antonio arrived in America, gas was readily available to the residents of Larimer for both outdoor street lights and indoor use. Water was heated in gas-fired boilers in the cellars of homes. The novelty of warm running water from faucets never wore off during Antonio's years in America. There was no running water cold or hot in the homes in Nicastro when he left. Antonio didn't know it but he had landed in an important place and time in America's, and in Pittsburgh's history.

A History Note-East Liberty/Larimer Avenue/Land of History

A little over 100 years before Antonio arrived, at about the time of the American Revolutionary War (from 1775-1783), East Liberty was open grazing land located in Allegheny County, Pennsylvania just a few miles east of the young town of Pittsburgh. In older English usage, a "liberty" was a plot of common land on the outskirts of a town.[40]

The land was owned by two patriarchs John Conrad Winebiddle and Alexander Negley. "Winebiddle owned land west of East Liberty in Bloomfield, Garfield and Friendship. Negley, a German settler, purchased a 278-acre farm north of East Liberty along the southern bank of the Allegheny River in 1778 which he named 'Fertile Bottom' and developed a village he named East Liberty after an old grazing commons. Negley's land included some of the present-day East Liberty and much of nearby Highland Park, Morningside, Larimer and Stanton Heights. Negley's son Jacob married Barbara Winebiddle and in 1799 purchased the 443-acre farm that adjoined his father's farm to the south and west. Jacob and Barbara built a manor house at the corner of Stanton and Negley Avenues in 1808 from which the substantial land holdings were managed when the two farms were combined upon the death of Alexander Negley in 1809. In 1816, Jacob Negley was a prominent citizen of the East Liberty Valley. He was instrumental in building the Pittsburgh-Greensburg Turnpike (Penn Avenue) through East Liberty which made the area a trading center and ensured its future growth."[41]

This was the road that followed the trail, called the Forbes Road, made by the British during the French and Indian War. Jacob Negley won the contract to pave a five-mile section of the Pittsburgh-Greenburg Turnpike between 1813 and 1819. He played a substantial role in founding the village of East Liberty and building a steam-powered grist mill on the turnpike in 1816. Jacob established a bank, and helped found the East Liberty Presbyterian Church in 1819.

His daughter Sarah Jane Negley's marriage to Thomas Mellon took place in that church in 1843.[42] Not long after the marriage, East Liberty began to develop as a commercial area. Sarah Jane's inherited fortune enabled Thomas Mellon, a lawyer, to sell and rent land near East Liberty and use the proceeds to finance Pittsburgh's industries. Mellon made his fortune through this marriage and the use of Negley's money. Mellon also saw the wisdom of making East Liberty a transportation hub and arranged for Pittsburgh's first trolley lines to pass through East Liberty in 1851. These were the transportation systems in place for Mellon when East Liberty was annexed in 1868.[43]

Larimer Avenue got its name long before Thomas Mellon came on the scene. The street was an old horse race track called Larimer Lane named after French-Scotsman William Larimer who owned a house and a Conestoga wagon business that hauled goods between Pittsburgh and Philadelphia between 1830 and 1850. The new railroad and station established by Mellon in East Liberty lured large numbers of German immigrants who later formed Saints Peter and Paul Church and School along Larimer Avenue.[44]

A History Note-Antonio's Travels Part of Immigrant History

"Come to America, there is opportunity here," was the word that spread back to the old country. Pittsburgh was one of the cities where that opportunity existed because of its industrial and commercial enterprises. There were jobs, there was opportunity and the Italians were not the only ones to see the possibilities. The area drew Russian and German born Polish immigrants. In addition, a significant number of African Americans, both foreign-born and southern-born, settled near the Larimer Village along Frankstown and Lincoln Avenues.[45] The next decade brought an additional number of southern-born African Americans escaping segregation and discrimination.[46] The Poles settled along the district's main arteries of Liberty and Penn Avenues. Austrian Poles arrived a decade later and settled in small clusters throughout the city. The Italians, who arrived toward the end of the 19th century, settled in what was called the Strip District Flood Plain along the Allegheny River. Newcomers most often resided for a short time with those responsible for their emigration.

America's industrialized cities were having major problems accommodating this flood of immigrants. Many were forced to live in deplorable conditions. In New York, for instance, they lived in tenements, sometimes five families in a 12 x 12 room with only two beds; no partitions, tables or chairs, no water or heat, and surrounded by vermin.[47] Immigrants who came to Pittsburgh faced living in squalor as conditions in Pittsburgh's Lower Hill district deteriorated. Those who did not have established family connections, who arrived earlier and moved to the Larimer Avenue Village area, started their American experiences harshly. Antonio was luckier than most. He had been informally adopted by his uncle and aunt who had already established themselves in the Larimer Avenue Village. His introduction was not uncomfortable and his comfort would be long lasting.

Sunday and Church

Ice-crystal coated windows told the story of blustery weather on Sunday morning as the Gaetano family prepared to go to Mass. Sunday in the Larimer Avenue Village was a day of rest for workers. Men worked 6 days a week, some from 8-12 hours a day depending on the type of work they did or for whom they worked. Rest was necessary to rejuvenate physically, emotionally and spiritually. Emotional rejuvenation was a natural for light-hearted Italians. Being with family... laughing...singing...talking in their native tongue...and eating, lots of eating, was the prescription. The Italians who were settling in the village of Larimer were Roman Catholic and going to Mass had the side benefit of bringing family and friends together. Domenico was anxious to take Antonio to Mass where he would meet others from his family and so many of Domenico and Maria's friends. Since Antonio arrived in America three years before the anchor Italian Church *'Our Lady Help of Christians Church'* was built on Meadow Street, Mass was being held in Bloomfield, in a blacksmith shop, and serviced by a traveling Italian priest. Italians of that time rejected the idea of attending Catholic Churches run by Irish or German Catholic Priests who did not speak their language. Not even the architectural beauty of its twin spirals or the magnificent stained glass windows of *'St. Peter and St. Paul's Roman Catholic Church'* sitting smack in the middle of the Italian community on Larimer Avenue enticed them. The reason was *'St. Peter and St. Paul's Church'* had been established as a mission of the Saint Philomena German Catholic Church from Pittsburgh's Strip District in 1890 to service local Catholics. The pressure to have an "Italian" Catholic Church had been building since 1894. Brought by the growing numbers of Italian Catholics,

Bishop Phelan finally granted permission to form a committee to finance the construction of *'Our Lady Help of Christian Church'*. This, the first Italian Catholic Church in Pittsburgh, was completed in 1898, three years after Antonio came to America. Eventually, the number of Italian speaking priests grew from one that made the rounds in 1895 to eleven by 1905 when the Italian church and all of its religious activities were well underway in Larimer.[48]

Our Lady Help of Christian Church

Attending Mass in a blacksmith shop was an informal sort of affair. The faithful stood or sat where they could, waiting for Father Salvadore Lagorio[49] to finish hearing confessions in an office at the back of the shop. Soon he began Mass and built to the crescendo...the consecration of the host and the renewal of faith for the faithful. The unity, the cohesiveness and the belonging were therapy for those who had resettled their lives so far from their roots. Catholicism was a binding force between immigrants and their nationality with priests playing a role that was beyond religious. As time progressed the priest became a dominant figure in the Italian community who had a voice in all things from birth to death. Since this was Father Lagorio's third and final Mass of the day, he took a moment to welcome Antonio as the newest immigrant to the group and using his thumb gave him a special blessing with the sign of the cross upon his forehead. Father Lagorio was from Calabria and knew of the Risorgimento. He was anxious to hear of relatives he had in the region and Antonio was happy to share what he knew. The Priest was not shy when talking about the effect Risorgimento had on the Papal States and the Pope's concerns. Shaking his head and gesturing with his arms he showed his distress and asked those attending Mass to pray for the church in their special intentions. He placed the chalice and the small gold container of remaining communion hosts in his black leather satchel. In his pocket he put the small cloth bag, now holding the Indian Head pennies given in support of the church, thanked the faithful and walked out the door.

After Mass it was on to Cousin Luigi's house to return the wool coat Domenico borrowed for Antonio to wear on his journey from Ellis Island. Antonio had given his Aunt Maria two of his twenty-five dollars to purchase enough wool cloth, 4 buttons and thread from the dry goods general store on Larimer Avenue to make him a warm coat. She had enough softer flannel cloth on hand to make the necessary layers within the coat. In the late 1800's the interior of a wool coat was layered with soft cloth for maximum warmth. Maria had a Singer foot peddle sewing machine she and Domenico had purchased a year before so she could take in sewing and make extra money for the family. It was with pride that Maria spoke of having the only Singer sewing machine in the neighborhood and her well known tailoring skills. She had requests to make communion dresses, coats and an occasional wedding dress. Most wedding and communion veils, finery, household cloths, rugs and doilies were hand sewn by women with extraordinary stitching skills. The plan was for Antonio to accompany Maria to purchase the coat materials and a pair of sturdy shoes on the avenue. The best shoes would cost 63 cents a pair and were sturdier than the pair that cost 56 cents. It was important for Antonio not to spend much of his money until he had secured a position and started working or Maria would have taken him shopping at Horne's Department Store at Penn Avenue and Stanwick Street in Downtown Pittsburgh.

The Family (La Famiglia)

La famiglia was then and is now the heart of the Italian culture. It was more than just natural to the culture. The family was the enclave within which the immigrant felt comfort while sharing language, familiar foods and religious practices. The language barrier made functioning outside the Italian speaking community confusing for men with marginal educations, and especially for the women who were illiterate. Home was the place to be nurtured and Sunday afternoon was the time to be with family.

This Sunday afternoon dinner visit had been planned at Luigi's apartment on Stoebner Way, just two blocks from Maxwell Way. As was customary Concette, Luigi's wife, prepared a large mid-day meal that would last at least 3 hours. Other cousins joined the group bringing with them their specialties in celebration of Antonio's arrival. There would be chicken soup; homemade spinach bread; hand churned butter; pepper, onion and egg frittatas bacala that had been soaking for two days in preparation for the feast, fresh vegetables of various types sautéed in olive oil and garlic; soft wheat pasta with an alfredo-like butter and cream sauce and home-made sausage. The rumors of tomatoes being poisonous had carried over from the old country. Tomatoes and spaghetti sauce or red gravy as it was called by some, would not become a staple in southern Italian cuisine until the early 1900's. The meal was accompanied by homemade Chianti wine (Vino) made nearby from grapes grown in what was known as Chianti Way. "Below the Meadow Street Bridge, a dirt road was named Chianti Way because of its Italian residents. This street was the main thoroughfare for the community called 'Basso La Vallone' or down the hollow'. Steps from Larimer Avenue led down to this small community of twenty-nine wooden structures. In some ways it was a rural community because residents cultivated vegetables and fruits, and raised livestock. A few Italians developed vineyards along the hills below Larimer, hence the name Chianti referred to the area."[50]

No gathering of Italians occurred without music. Cousin Carmine brought his mandolin and others their operatic voices. As was customary, after dinner and before song, the men gathered in one area and the women in the other. Children climbed from lap to lap, from aunt to uncle, from mama to papa. The men talked of their work and the world. The women talked of sewing, cooking and the antics of their children. Men shared information in letters received from the old country. Luigi asked if Domenico had arranged for an interview for Antonio at the gas company. "Si," Domenico answered, "There is work." Since Antonio was already 15-years-old, he would have no trouble getting the working papers needed to be accepted as an employee of the gas company. He was sure Antonio would be hired much like Maria's cousin Giovanni had been hired on Domenico's recommendation. Domenico had talked to his boss about giving Antonio a job when he knew Antonio made up his mind to come to America.

It was customary for established Italians to care for newcomers from the homeland and that included taking advantage of the relationship a working man had with this employer. Italians were solid, dependable workers and when one worker's friend or family member was in need of a job, a job would be available for the 'Paesano'. The wintery Sunday was coming to a close. After some song and a combination of both light and heavy deserts, it was time for home and the warm bed Antonio and his very full stomach welcomed.

Shopping and Learning the Neighborhood
The next day Domenico left the apartment for work before dawn. At nine in the morning, Antonio and Maria made their way past the construction site of the new Larimer Avenue Public School to the dry goods store. The closed-wall shops intrigued Antonio. In Italy, the

shops were open sided until the rains came. The shops then closed and everyone went home. Here the shops were open all day, with fixed hours no matter what the weather. Shoes lined the walls of the dry goods store and bolts of cloth were stacked on broad wooden counters.

It was not long before Antonio chose a pair of high-topped leather shoes, with Maria's guidance. These shoes cost 63 cents and by far were the best ones for Antonio. The shop had no boots; but, Maria said if Antonio got the job at the gas company they would provide the boots he would need for work. Maria picked the wool cloth, buttons and thread to make Antonio's warm coat. His pants and shirts would be purchased when Antonio had enough money to purchase his own. In the meantime, he would wear Domenico's work pants and shirts. Antonio purchased a cap for 81 cents after Maria talked him out of buying the "high-styled" fur hat for $1 he really wanted. He also bought gloves for 14 cents; two pair of men's cotton hose at 10 cents each; soft-cotton, full-body underwear for 72 cents and a much-needed razor for 38 cents.[51]

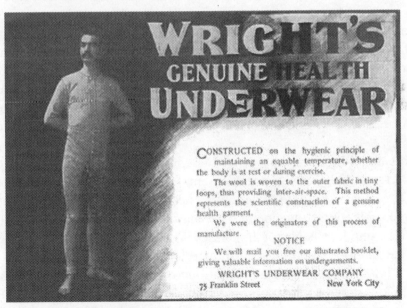

Advertisement of typical men's long underware worn in 1895 and most probably what Antonio bought for warmth

By the time they left the shop, the street had filled with women doing their daily shopping. Small children clung to their mothers' skirts as they walked. Horse drawn wagons brought supplies to several stores on the Avenue. The pair paused to let a streetcar pass, dodging other horse and wagons hauling various things. The winter sun was welcomed as Maria stopped at the grocery shop to pick up 2 lbs. of codfish for 6 cents, a lemon for 2 cents, and a pound of coffee for 10 cents.[52] Antonio eyed the stick candy and licorice. He bought 3 pieces of stick candy at 1 cent each as a special after dinner treat for his new family in appreciation for all they were doing for him. Balancing their bundles, they made their way back to Maxwell Avenue and the warm apartment that awaited them.

In the afternoon the fittings began. Maria laid newspaper on the floor of the living room to make the pattern for the coat. She told Antonio to lay down on the newspaper. He laid on his back with his arm extended while she drew his shape on the paper. As he stood up, she wrapped her oil-cloth tape measure around his waist, measured the length of his arms, the breadth of his shoulders, and the height from his neck to just above his calf carefully noting the numbers. Maria could not read much; but, Domenico taught her to read numbers and the words she would need. He felt it was necessary if her sewing would bring money into the household. Maria was not only a quick study, she also had nimble fingers and a knack for creating good-looking garments. Antonio was in good hands. Time passed quickly. Soon it would be 6 o'clock and Vincenzo would be home. Food preparation had to begin for the man who worked all day.

The Job/The Company

Domenico set the appointment for Antonio's interview with Mr. Vecchio. Antonio, wearing his new long underwear, shoes and socks felt confident as he met the man who would be his new boss. This confident behavior impressed Mr. Vecchio and Antonio was scheduled to start work the following Monday.

Early in America's economic recovery from the depression of 1893, Antonio could expect to make about $1.50 a day or $9.00 for a 6-day week as a beginner common laborer. The wage could go to $10.50 a week as his skill increased.

Working for the gas company as a skilled laborer was one of the higher paying jobs at the time. There was stability at the company and the potential of becoming a foreman.

Pittsburgh was a mecca for skilled construction jobs for brick layers, stone masons & plasterers for large commercial buildings, schools, government buildings and churches. Also, there were jobs installing gas and sewer lines, and paving streets. There were jobs in steel mills that paid $12.95 a week for those who knew carpentry or had learned to make the steel rails for streetcars and trains.

Skilled workers in Pittsburgh's steel mills made the materials that generated jobs for unskilled laborers. Triggered by the depression, unskilled jobs paid far less particularly after the unions were broken by Andrew Carnegie and other captains of industry.

A 12-hour-day was established with wages in the mills tumbling down to $11.88 per week for a 12-hour-day, six-days a week. For some unskilled jobs workers were paid just 3 cents an hour was paid with some earning 36 cents for a 12-hour day. Workers were pushed to the point of exhaustion and accidents resulting in death were frequent. Coupled with the lack of safety regulations, it was the worst of times for the immigrant mill worker.[53]

The recession's impact on the working class was devastating. Unemployment climbed to 20% in 1894. Close to 2.5 million jobless men migrated in and out of American cities looking for work. Domenico fully understood the depression as he could see the influx of jobless workers searching for employment. He made sure he demonstrated loyalty and diligence to his boss Mr. Vecchio and did what he could to keep his job during the economic downturn. His loyalty protected Antonio and who too young and inexperienced in American ways to fully realize what trouble the United States was in.

Industrialist and investor George Westinghouse, who had acquired Domenico's employer, the Equitable Gas Company, had folded it into what was now the Philadelphia Company. Positioning the company to prosper, he extending its operations into the production, transportation and distribution of natural gas in Pittsburgh.

Conveniently enough, a sizable natural gas field was found in the rear yard of Westinghouse's home in East Pittsburgh, just five years after natural gas was discovered while drilling for oil in the Pittsburgh suburb of Murraysville, PA. It is said Westinghouse was not a man to miss an opportunity to advance his industrial holdings. He immediately created a company that would bring natural gas to every business and residence in the greater Pittsburgh area, capitalizing on Pittsburgh's reputation of becoming the industrial center of the United States.

Because, natural gas was becoming the ideal fuel for industrial and residential applications, was not eager to lay off skilled laborers as the demand for gas was strong even if the economy was weak. The quicker gas lines could be laid, the quicker the return on investment. Users of gas...cities to light their streets; homeowners to cook and heat water; and industry for the production of glass, chemicals, paint and steel needed massive amounts of fuel for heat and were willing to pay for it. Miles of piping were needed to transport the gas from wellhead to end user; and gas meters were needed to measure its use. Westinghouse invented a more secure type of pipe joint and a device that automatically cut the flow of gas to a home or business in which a leak had developed. Westinghouse had little trouble convincing Pittsburgh's City Council that he could deliver gas safely to the Pittsburgh area.[54]

Westinghouse's extended reach into the development of electricity branched out his economic base long before his experiments in Alternating Current Electricity (AC) with Nicola Testla lit up the 1893 Chicago World's Fair introducing the country to electricity.

Antonio Listens and Learns

By the time Antonio made his way home from the interview, the sewing of his new coat had begun. It would take three days. Until then, the long underwear coupled with Domenico's layered work shirts and pants would have to do. Tuesday-Saturday, Domenico worked, came home to a hot bath and Maria's warm dinners. Antonio took the time to learn about the neighborhood picking up a newspaper every morning on the Avenue at a cost of 2 cents each. He helped Maria where he could. He organized his money. He thought about his future and the seaside life he left behind in Nicastro. Arriving in America in the dead of winter was somewhat of a shock and required an adjustment for Antonio.

Even though he was surrounded by Italian speaking people, he knew nothing about his newly adopted country. As he walked on the

Avenue he heard people talking about life outside the community. Some spoke of the prejudice they had experienced. He didn't understand because everything was strange to this 15-year-old. He felt uneasy more times than not, especially when he heard those stories. He felt if he was to succeed, he would have to learn to read, write and understand the *(American)* language. The most available and inexpensive learning tools were the newspapers and magazines being printed at the time. It has been said these periodicals were an "indirect Americanization school for the immigrant..." Of the five newspapers and two magazines the *"Unione"* and *"La Trinacria"*, and the *"Vita"* (a religious publication printed by the United Presbyterian church) were available for national news and the other two contained the news of the Pittsburgh Italian communities.[55] Antonio's literacy put him a step ahead of fellow countrymen in the Larimer Avenue Village. He learned to read, write, and speak in broken English quickly. He also learned the English used by many immigrants to get along in other Italian dialect speaking neighborhoods and stores. Italians of that time created a language of their own in which all dialects became infused with Americanisms. This new language was neither Italian nor English, and often was only intelligible to the Italian immigrants. The language included the words *'jiobba'* for job; *'grossiera'* for grocery; *'basso'* for boss; *'marachetta'* for market; *'baccausa'* for outhouse; *'ticchetto'* for ticket; *'bisiniss'* for business; *'trocco'* for truck; *'sciabola'* for shovel; *'loffare'* for the verb to loaf; *'carpetto'* for carpet and *'masura'* meant for sure.[56] Sunday came around quickly and within his first week in America Antonio had his new warm coat which he wore to Sunday Mass. The family gathering after Mass was at cousin Angela and Giuseppe Antonucci's house. Maria basked in the compliments on her handwork in Antonio's new coat as the noisy bunch enjoyed each other that afternoon.

Antonio and The Progressive Era

America was in the second year of an economic recovery when Antonio stepped foot on its shores in 1895. The depression was considered the worst in the nation's history. A surge of stock selling rocked a stock market already unsettled by the spectacular failure of the Philadelphia and Reading Railroad in February of 1893. Approximately fifty railroads had gone under and chaos erupted since this industry was one of the nations largest and supported other industries. The ripple effect collapsed more than thirty steel companies.[(57)]

The government struggled to cope with the crisis and stemmed the outflow of its gold supply. In 1895 it also secured emergency loans in gold from Wall Street syndicates including $65 million from John Pierpont Morgan and his associates. The government paid $70 million for this bailout.[(58)] Economic recovery came slowly for the US and would not stabilize until the middle of 1897.[(59)]

Even if Antonio's years were filled with the hardness of earning a small sum as a laborer, he enjoyed those formative years in America. The excitement of earning & saving money and living freely was encouraging. By February of 1896, he began contributing $1.50 a month to Domenico and Maria for his room and board plus buying an occasional special treat for them. By 1902, in less than 7 years, Antonio's wages increased from $78 a year to $83.20 a year. He was able to save $3.26 a month after his expenses. He used 5 cents a day for streetcar fare or 30 cents a week if he bought a weekly pass, paid his room and board, and contributed 4 cents a month to the church. He still had the remainder of his original $25 left after buying material for his coat and other items. He banked $3 every month and since there were no income taxes in those days every penny he made he could keep.[(60)] His passbook savings account at the First National Bank in Pittsburgh grew. He made many friends with others his age in the village. By the time he turned 22 years old in 1917, Antonio had grown and prospered in this Italian community as it grew and prospered in America's *'Progressive Era'*.[(61)]

Antonio Gaetano at 22 years

A History Note-The Evolution of the Larimer Avenue East Liberty Village; the State of Pennsylvania and State of the Nation during the Progressive Era.

The Evolution of the Larimer Avenue, East Liberty Village

While Antonio was growing up, construction of Larimer Avenue School on one acre of land at Larimer Avenue and Winslow Street had concluded in 1896 and was topped off with its famous clock tower reminiscent to those in Calabria.

Our Lady Help of Christian Catholic Church had been built on Meadow Street in 1898 after that prolonged battle between the Diocese of Pittsburgh and growing numbers of Italian Catholics who wanted their own parish.

The 380-acre Highland Park opened to the public in 1893 and the Highland Park Zoo opened its doors in 1897 to the delight of hundreds of visitors.

Shops expanded along Larimer Avenue and included bread stores like Stagno's, Pastry shops like Moio's that sold cannoli, pastaciotti, and the unique and memorable lemon ice treat in a paper cone perfect for hot summer nights in the city. Grocery stores specializing in old world foods enabled Italians to continue their traditional culinary delights using olive oil, pasta, cheeses and meats like fresh sweet or hot Italian sausage. Bacala, Clamare and Smeltz, preserved in salt, were stuffed inside wooden barrels parked on store front sidewalks. [62] The Hurdy-Gurdy man paraded up and down Larimer Avenue amusing children while he made a penny or two.

In 1900, Kingsley House was a staple of the East Liberty community. Operators of Kingsley House were university graduates who believed forming partnerships with the community as an equal participant, and sharing its issues and concerns, would bring solutions to the new problems of urban life for immigrants. It was a facility that became key to the social growth of the immigrant community. Kingsley House provided cultural, educational, and social programming; boy's and girl's clubs; literary societies; lectures; concerts; kindergarten; and science and reading classes. The facility grew as a result of the industrial revolution and poor immigrant workers from the mills and factories who were in tremendous need. Initially located in the old Montooth Mansion at Bedford and Fullerton Streets in Pittsburgh's Hill District, the organization expanded to Larimer Avenue in 1923.[63]

Evolution of the State of Pennsylvania & the State of the Nation.
Between the end of the Civil War in April of 1865 and the economic down turn in 1894, rapid economic development laid the groundwork for a modern U.S. industrial economy. Industrialists Andrew Carnegie in Steel; George Westinghouse in Gas and Electricity; J. Pierpont Morgan in banking; Jay Gould in Railroads and John D. Rockefeller in Oil, whose drive for success, power and fame, all moved the country forward. It was the golden age of capitalism with a focus on greed and money. An array of discovery occurred in the late 19th century in what was known as the 'Gilded Age'. Oil was found in PA. Elsewhere in the country the typewriter, telephone, phonograph, electric light and refrigerated railroad cars became available. The disposable razor made its debut by the Gillette Co. That patented the first one.[64] Cars began to replace the horse and carriage. People were flying in airplanes. Coal was found in abundance in the Appalachian Mountains from PA south to Kentucky. Large iron mines opened

30

in the Lake Superior region of the upper midwest. Mills thrived in places were these two important raw materials could be brought together to produce steel. Large copper and silver mines opened, followed by lead mines and cement factories. These were major changes and growth in the nation's industrial infrastructure.

Newcomers to business like Frederick W. Taylor pioneered the field of scientific management in the late 19th century by developing mass production methods. He carefully plotted the functions of various workers and then devised new, more efficient ways for them to do their jobs. As a result, in 1913, Henry Ford was inspired to develop the moving assembly line. Each worker did one simple task in the production of automobiles. Ford was ingenious in more than one way. He offered a generous wage of $5 a day to his workers. That wage enabled many of his employees to buy the automobiles they made, helping the industry to expand and Ford's profits to increase.

This explosion of new discoveries and inventions caused profound changes in what was called a "second industrial revolution". This was a revolution in which no one was battling for the working class. The gap between the rich and the poor grew at a rapid rate and newly minted Americans rode this bucking bronco with the strength of their conviction and their belief that the decision to make their fortune in this country was a correct one. While it was rough riding in their parallel universe, immigrants learned that seeing a long-range potential for a new service or product was the way the rich amassed their vast financial empires. Immigrants applied the knowledge of the rich and enthusiastically embraced the idea of making money. It was the risk and the excitement of business enterprise, higher living standards, and the potential rewards of power brought by success that motivated them.

The three titans of industry, Messers. Carnegie, Morgan and Rockefeller were determined to hold on to their control of industry and their success as the presidential election of 1896 approached. Democratic candidate William Jennings Bryan campaigned on a platform of breaking up their companies by forcing anti-trust legislation that would make monopolies illegal. He did it because of the poor working conditions being forced on employees of their companies. In a rare unification act, these normally competitive titans pulled their money to "buy a president" who would support their interests and allow them to remain in control of their businesses and their control of whole segments of the country's industry. By outspending Bryan by 5-1, their $600,000 investment (nearly one billion in 2015 dollars) and campaign insured the win of their candidate, a Republican from Ohio named William McKinley. That money bought a four year extension of their control on America's industrial foundations. However, as fate would have it, President William McKinley was shot by a Polish-American anarchist Leon Czolgosz while shaking hands at the Pan American Exposition in Buffalo, N.Y. on September 14, 1901. The assassination propelled the progressive Vice President Theodore Roosevelt into the White House as the 26th President of the United States. There would be critical changes in American businesses in his more than eight years in office. "Roosevelt was an energized political reformer who infused the executive office with the same frenetic energy that characterized his entire life. From the start he was committed to make government work for the people and in many respects the people living in burgeoning ethnic enclaves never needed the government more. He championed legislation regulating railroads, interstate commerce, labor and the food and drug industries among his many other contributions to the country."[65]

As the American economy matured, a crucial change came. It was the emergence of corporations that first appeared in the railroad industry.[66] Other changes included the "Pittsburgh Post Gazette" making its debut by printing a daily newspaper in 1901. In 1906, it changed its name to the "Gazette Times". Readers learned of worldly events like Butch Cassidy & the Sundance Kid robbing a train of $40,000 in Wagner, Montana; and, Pablo Picasso opening his first art exhibition in Paris in 1901. More importantly, they learned about business and any potential changes being contemplated for the Village.

The early 1900's saw nearly all Larimer Avenue Italian immigrants, who had come to America since Ellis Island opened in 1892, advance their status. Many were able to save a portion of their earnings for their future. The Italian community was solidly established with schools, shops, churches and transportation in place. Jobs by that time had become plentiful, the community had survived the depression of 1893, and the progressive area, with Teddy

Roosevelt leading the charge, was at a full gallop. Progressives in the country believed that family was the foundation of American society and the government, especially municipal government, was to work to strengthen and enhance it. Local public assistance programs were reformed to try to keep families together. Special emphasis was put on pure milk and water supplies. State and national new food and drug laws were created to strengthen efforts to guarantee a safe food system.[67]

It was into this progressive America, and the solidly anchored Larimer Avenue Village, that Giuseppe Gallippi made his entrance in 1903. His was not a direct, nor an easy path.

CHAPTER 2

VOYAGER GIUSEPPE GALLIPPI
(September 26, 1875 – June 25, 1929)

Giuseppe's Life Before Coming to America

Giuseppe Gallippi was the second son of **Antonio Teti & Caterina LaFicara,** of Filogaso, Vibo Valentia, in the Province of Reggae de Calabria, Italy. *(See the Gallippi family tree on page 36)* In 1875, when Giuseppe was born, economic conditions in southern Italy, as stated earlier, were dismal. His parents struggled to put food on the table for him and his older brother **Antonio.** Nearly all the families in Filogaso openly supported each other for survival.

Remember, *'Risorgimento' (1860-1870)* had changed Italy, impoverishing its southern provinces leaving economic ruin in its path. There was no transportation nor were there any industries that could provide work for its people.

Giuseppe's father Antonio and the Gallippi family were creative business people. They were able to take advantage of a specific situation created by the Italian government. The government would lease undeveloped forested lands for business purposes but would not allow the purchase of those lands. Government inspectors insured all the trees would not be cut from the land by marking the ones that were to remain. The Gallippi family leased several hundred acres of wooded land from the government and became brokers of materials grown on sections of the wooded property. The Gallippi men would make arrangements with small business owners to harvest the trees for use as building lumber, firewood and charcoal made from wood scraps left after the harvest. The products were then sold and monies from the sales would be shared. The lumber brokerage business along with their involvement in the production of olive oil from the abundance of olive trees in the area sustained the family.

Giuseppe became an expert on the cultivation of olive trees and soil preparation. At his father's side, he learned about the production of olive oil. There certainly was a demand for olive oil as cooking with this product was part of the Italian cuisine. However, very few people had enough money to purchase the product, so the Gallippi family used it as a form of currency to purchase or barter for the items they needed.

Honesty was a family trait. Giuseppe's brother Antonio's grave marker in the Filogaso cemetery carries the inscription *'Commerciante Onestissimo'* – translation 'Honest Businessman' - 'Born 1867- Died 1931'.

Economic struggles brought tensions. Family recollections indicate Giuseppe and his brother Antonio did not have a good relationship. Before long, Antonio left for Argentina to work on the coffee plantations. There was no further communication between the brothers.

Antonio's two sons **Peppino** and **Antonio,** and their mother **Arena Gelormina** remained in Filogaso. Throughout his adult life, their father, Antonio, traveled back and forth from Argentina to Italy as did other men of that time. Antonio's son Peppino married **Contello;** and, his son Antonio married **Agatha.** Peppino soared to great heights in the community by first becoming a lawyer and then the Mayor of Filogaso. Peppino and Contello had no children; however, Antonio and Agatha had four children. They were **Gelormina,** who died early; **Sarina,** who immigrated to Argentina; **Rachela,** who, at this writing, lives in Filogaso, and **Antonio,** who eventually emigrated to Pittsburgh. Filogaso, then as now, is a town with a population of approximately 1,200 people who make up the 400 families living there. It is a town of residences, churches, schools, farms, orange trees and olive groves. Today as then, there are few opportunities to work and earn enough money to support a family.

Gallippi, Giuseppe Family Tree

(Great Grandparents)
Antonio Gallippi + Caterina Laficara

(Grandparents)
Giuseppe Gallippi married Maria Catarina Teti
(1875-1929)

Antonio Gallippi married **Arena Gilorama**
(1867-1931)

Antonio married **Agatha**
(Emigrated to Pittsburgh –lived with our Grandma)

Giuseppe (called Peppino) married **Contello**
(Peppino was a lawyer and the Mayor of Filogaso.)
(There were no children.)

Rachela
(Has homes in Milano and Filogaso.
Has one daughter who is a lawyer
and three granddaughters.)

Antonio
(Emigrated to Pgh.
eventually moved
to Florida.)

Gelormina
(Died early.)

Sarina
(Emigrated to Argentina)

Victoria	Antonina	Antonio	Vincenzo	Rosalia	Almina	Virginia	Benedetto	Emilio	Adalina
Feb 6, 1900	Dec 6, 1906	May 26, 1908	Nov 1, 1909	Jan 25, 1911	Apr 18, 1913	Jan 11, 1915	Oct 5, 1916	Dec 16, 1918	Jan 14, 1920
1985	1981	1987	1991	2011	2008	2009	1999	2001	2001

The History of Filogaso

The earliest written accounts of Filogaso date back to 950 AD when this small hamlet stood next to another hamlet called Panajia. There is a history of these hamlets being attacked and plundered by the *'Saracens'*, a name used by the ancient Greeks and Romans to describe the Arab tribes that threatened their borders. The two hamlets became part of one province and ownership eventually landed in the hands of King Ferdinand II of Spain. This King was the Catholic who gave the fief of Filogaso to Gurello Carafa in exchange for the city of Newfoundland. Carafa built his palace in Filogaso and lived there. In 1523, a convent called Santa Maria di Loreto was founded by a Dominican named *'Friar Vincenzo from the Grotteria'*. It is said relics of Jesus Christ's cross were kept in the convent. The convent also served as a *'cemetery of sacred grounds'* where various Dukes and other nobles were buried. *(A clarification is necessary. There is a street in Filogaso named "Via Gallippi". It was thought that street was named after our Gallippi family; however, after further research, it was not. There is another family named Gallippi living in Filogaso, and one of its members has been honored by naming a street after him. Also, in the cemetery there are many descendants of that Gallippi family whose names and faces appear on their tomb stones. To add to the complication, families named their children after themselves, first and last names, generation after generation, and in some cases married their relatives making it difficult to understand which generation to which Antonio, Giuseppe, Caterina or Lucrezia belonged.)*

A street sign in modern Filogaso, Italy

Cemetery marker of other Gallippi family in Filogaso

Typical modern street in Filogaso

Giuseppe Gallippi and Maria Catarina Teti Marry

It was 1898 when Grandpa Giuseppe, then 23-years-old, fancied a lovely member of the Teti family, our Grandmother Maria Catarina Teti. She was 19-years-old and ready for Giuseppe's displays of affection after he asked permission of her father to court her. By all accounts, this was not an arranged marriage as many were in southern Italy's small towns. It was a genuine attraction of two people who were well suited for each other and whose affection for each other helped them weather the long separation they would endure in what would become a part of their life-long relationship. With the blessings of both families, Giuseppe and Maria Catarina courted for a year and married in January of 1899. Their first daughter, Victoria was born on February 11, 1900. No matter how hard or how creative the Gallippi family and the Teti's were, there were not enough ways to earn a living in southern Italy. Most southern Italian men were forced to seek income in other countries that they would send to Italy to support their families. Giuseppe felt his responsibility to support his wife and child was paramount. In 1900, less than a year after Victoria was born, and as Giuseppe turned 25, he was on his way to Brazil in search of opportunity and a living wage.

Giuseppe and Brazil

Giuseppe had grown up with the idea that South America was the land of opportunity. Brazil had been putting out the welcome mat to countries in the world encouraging emigration since the early 1800's. In 1819, the first group of immigrants arrived in Brazil from Switzerland and settled in Rio de Janeiro. Germans arrived later in 1824 settling in Rio Grande de Sul; Ukrainians and Pols settled in Parana; Turks and Arabs settled in Amazonia, and the Italians settled in San Paulo along with the Japanese and Spaniards. [68] The influx of European emigration to Brazil was inspired by the rise of abolitionism when the Emperor of Brazil issued a proclamation stating it would be unlawful to continue to carry on the African slave trade. That order came in 1830; and was pretty much ignored by coffee plantations owners. The Brazilian government did not push the issue as the export of coffee was expected to provide the lucrative income needed to sustain the country for the next 140 years.[69]

In 1888, when Giuseppe was 10-years-old, Brazil finally abolished slavery after a history of using African slaves since the mid-16th century. Slave labor was the driving force behind Brazil's growth of the sugar economy; the mining of gold and diamonds; cattle ranching; food stuff production; and coffee growing and production. In fact, when Brazil abolished slavery, it was the last country in the western world to do so and it was done a full 15 years after slavery was abolished through the 13th amendment to the United States Constitution in December of 1865. In Brazil's long history of slavery, an estimated four million slaves were imported from Africa to Brazil, or 40% of the total number of slaves brought to the Americas, both north and south. In anticipation of losing slave labor, coffee growers and the Brazilian government experimented with alternative labor schemes to support their economic interests. The country was constantly seeking ways to fill the need for workers and attractive offers were made to encourage European emigration to San Paulo. Seaports were opened, emigration laws were relaxed and immigrants arrived by the thousands to work on coffee plantations as laborers for what they felt would be opportunities for land ownership.[70]

At first, Brazilian coffee plantation owners enticed European immigrants by offering to pay for their transportation; giving them a house and land to grow their own food and assigning a specific number of coffee trees to tend, harvest, and process. The catch was that the sharecroppers had to pay off the debt they incurred for the transportation costs, along with other advances. Since it was illegal for the immigrants to move off the plantation until all debts were repaid, which typically took years, this amounted to debt peonage, another form of slavery. The practice abated somewhat when the 'paulista farmers" finally gained enough political clout to persuade the Brazilian government to pay for immigrants' transportation costs, so that new laborers did not arrive with a pre-existing debt burden. However, they still incurred debt as they paid to live there and rent land. They were called 'Colonos' and were mostly poor Italians who came to work on San Paulo plantations between 1884 and 1914.[71]

Giuseppe landed in San Paulo to work on a coffee plantation as did more than a million other immigrants. Some 'Colonos' eventually managed to secure their own land. Others earned just enough to return to their homelands, embittered and discouraged. Because of the poor working and living conditions, most plantations maintained a band of *'Capangas'* or armed guards who carried out the plantation owners will.[72] No confirming documentation was found to prove whether Giuseppe's passage was paid by the Brazilian government under the new rule; or whether his debt included his passage. It is reasonable to speculate he stayed in Brazil, working under what could have been deplorable conditions for three years. It took that long to pay whatever debt he had before leaving San Paulo, Brazil in 1903. We do know those dreams of land ownership were not realized in Brazil. He decided his best opportunity for progress would be to go to North America. Through a cousin by marriage named Giuseppe Rizzo, arrangements were made to sponsor Giuseppe's emigration to America and to live with him in the Larimer Avenue Village.

Giuseppe Gallippi Arrives in America in 1903

A tide of immigrants came in waves to America's shore, year after year, steamship after steamship. They came from Germany, Poland, Lithuania, Brazil, France, England and Italy arriving at Ellis Island in the thousands and dispersing to several key industrialized cities of which Pittsburgh was one. Industry was providing work opportunities. Italian families had established themselves and were welcoming "paesans" who wanted to emigrate to America. One such voyage carried our grandfather, 28-year-old Giuseppe Gallippi.

Giuseppe saved the $15 for his passage to N.Y. He boarded the steamship *"SS CapFrio"* from the Brazilian Port of Santos, in San Paulo, Brazil on March 30, 1903 arriving at Ellis Island on April 10, 1903. He was a small man "weighing 125 lbs. with brown hair and brown eyes and no distinctive marks" so according to his naturalization application papers said. Other sources were used to document Giuseppe's voyage. First, were his naturalization papers that referred to his arrival at Ellis Island on April 10, 1903 on the ship listed as the *"Capre"*. *(Note: Naturalization papers can be viewed in Chapter 3)*

Giuseppe Gallippi at 35 years old in 1910

The handwriting was unclear and it is common knowledge that many names were misunderstood or misspelled due to the language barriers between the immigrant and the person writing the document. To compound matters, many steamships at that time had changed ownership or names, and were chartered or sailed under different names in subsequent voyages. Tracing the name of the ship resulted in the discovery that the *"SS CapFrio"* was originally the *"SS Antonina"* built by the Blohm & Voss Company and launched by the Hamburg South America Steamship Fleet in 1898 as one of its Heritage Ships. Its name changed to the *"SS CapFrio"* when it was chartered by HAPAG in 1900. This ship regularly sailed from South America to Ellis Island, N.Y. Further confirmation came from a New York Times news clipping announcing the arrival of two steamships of the Hamburg-America Line that were scheduled to land at Ellis Island with immigrants in steerage. *"On the red letter day in April 1903, 10,236 aliens arrived in New York, and two steamers of the Hamburg-American line brought 2,731 and 2,854 steerage on a single trip"*. The article indicated that 1,100 immigrants came from South America on one of the ships.[73] These two ships were the only ships landing at Ellis in April of 1903, and since Giuseppe arrived on April 10, 1903, the presumption is this was Giuseppe's ship.

Giuseppe Gallippi was not a single 'Sojourner' like 15-year-old Antonio Gaetano was when he made his first voyage to America. Giuseppe was married and had not seen his wife or child since he sailed from Filogaso to Brazil three years before. After establishing himself in America, Giuseppe sailed to Filogaso to reunite with his family for the first time in five years. It was 1905 and he returned to America that same year to work and make arrangements to bring Maria Catarina and 6-year old Victoria to live in America in 1906.

A History Note-America Coping with Increased Immigration

In the early 1900's, there were many factors causing the US government to look at modifying the immigration laws. There was the assassination of President McKinley and President Roosevelt's address to congress requesting the exclusion and deportation of anarchist immigrants. He said, "I earnestly recommend to the Congress that in the exercise of its wise discretion it should take into consideration the coming to this country of anarchists or persons professing principles hostile to all government...they and those like them should be kept out of this country; and if found here should be promptly deported to the country from whence they came."

Immigration law changed on March 3, 1903. By the time the bill wound its way through both houses of Congress, it included four inadmissible classes: anarchists, people with epilepsy, beggars, and importers of prostitutes.[74] It is not hard to see the stretch in logic banning anarchists from coming into this country, even though the assassination of McKinley was carried out by an American-born son of polish immigrants... and not an actual immigrant. There was even logic in banning importers of prostitutes and maybe beggars, although I'm not sure about the criteria used to determine what classified a person as a beggar. But, why people with epilepsy were included in the group, unfortunately, was most probably based on ignorance, superstition and fear.

The law made little impact. Commissioner-General of Immigration Frank P. Sargent reported that from the time the law took effect in 1903 until June 30, 1914, a total of 15 anarchists were denied entry to the U.S.; four were expelled in 1913 and three in 1914.[75] Because the change in immigration law passed only about one month before Giuseppe arrived, and because the bureaucracy moved as slowly then as it does now; it was business as usual when he arrived in America and was processed at Ellis Island in the same way Antonio Gaetano was processed. Giuseppe, of course, was not an anarchist, nor did he meet any of the other criteria that would have blocked his entry into America. He was one of the 1,000,000 people who immigrated to America in 1903.

Sargent wrote, this was the largest number of people to emigrate and be added to America's population in one year in the history of immigration to America. His report showed 75% were in the unskilled class, designated as "laborers" or with "no occupation". [76]

Sargent felt those officers charged with inspecting incoming *"aliens"* were not diligent enough and many undesirables were entering the country. He also felt the country should stop the flow of the unskilled as they were not adding anything to the country and there would be "serious bearing" on the well-being of the country. His report also contained some interesting facts. It showed in 1903, of the total of 857,046 steerage aliens, 613,146 were males and 243,900 were females, of whom 102,431 were less than 14 years of age; and 714,053 ranged in age from 14 to 45; and 40,562 were 45 years old and over.[77] "There were of these 3,341 who could read but not write, and 185,667 who could neither read nor write, leaving a balance of 668,038 able to both read and write. It also appears that 76,702 of these steerage aliens had been in the United States before; that 128,266 of them each brought $30 in money or more; that 511,302 had each less than $30, and that the total amount of money shown by them to the officers was $16,117,513."[78]

Steamship companies saw this desire to get to America as a boon to their bottom line. Competition took over and steerage rates were cut on trips from English and Scottish ports to New York, to $10 from the $25 being paid for that voyage. However, the law required more diligence by steamship companies forbidding them to advertise except in the most perfunctory way, and it subjected them to a fine of $1,000 for every illegal immigrant they attempted to land at Ellis Island. All ship owners were required to make out complete manifests of all passengers on ships traveling to America. These included

44

answers to many questions concerning their physical, mental and financial status. Ship owners became responsible for returning all deported or rejected immigrants and for paying the expense of their maintenance while in the U.S. The U.S. Government sent Marcus Braun to southeastern Europe to investigate steamship companies' activities regarding immigrants. He reported the law was working well. He also reported, "The Italian government was in constant fear that the United States may pass laws against Italian immigration, which would be a serious thing for Italy, as whole towns in the southern part are supported mainly by remittances (wages) from American workers."[79] Mr. Braun also reported the Italian authorities had imprisoned several of the most notorious steamship 'runners'. All over Europe it was generally understood it was no easy thing to get into the United States.[80]

Giuseppe Lands at Ellis Island

Grandpa Giuseppe, unlike Grandpa Antonio Gaetano, saw the majestic Statue of Liberty standing high over New York Harbor as his welcome to America. The possessions of this worn man were meager and easily handled as he boarded the barge for the short trip to Ellis Island. Giuseppe was not surprised at the regimen to get through the entrance process as he had heard of it from many others who had emigrated to the United States before him. The warm shower and the relief of clean clothing against his body began the comforting process. The physical examination posed no problems and the 'eye man' found no disease in Giuseppe's eyes. He was too tired to have the anxiety of others when finding his place in the long **'Primary Line'** awaiting the now customary 29 questions to be asked of him. His papers were in order with his sponsor Rizzo's name clearly visible and he had the required $25. Giuseppe was handed his **'Landing Cards',** escorted to the **'Money Exchange'** and on to the **'Kissing Room'** where Rizzo was waiting. Giuseppe Rizzo had travelled from the Larimer Avenue Village to greet Giuseppe and the greeting was a warm, long-awaited embrace. "We will write to Filogaso as soon as we get to the Larimer Village so Catarina will know of your arrival," said Rizzo. Giuseppe held onto his paesan for a long moment. His eyes teared as he was at once filled with relief at the end of his long journey and concern about facing a new beginning. The 12-hour train ride to Pittsburgh was filled with talk of the family punctuated by frequent naps, and bits of cheese and bread. Finally they boarded the streetcar in East Liberty for the remaining trip to Larimer Avenue and Giuseppe's new home.

Cool spring air wrapped itself around Giuseppe as he stepped down the two-stair exit from the streetcar into the bustle of activity at Larimer Avenue and Meadow Street. To Giuseppe it seemed the street was alive with energy. Swishing skirts of ladies holding their childrens' hands, horse-drawn wagons clopping along, grocers talking in a language Giuseppe understood with animated gestures to patrons at sidewalk displays of fruits and vegetables. It was the village he had heard about and not a plantation armed with guards and false promises. He saw freedom in action and liked it. After his grueling and often lonely years in San Paulo, his goal was to bring his family to this village in America. The cool spring season in Pittsburgh was a shocking contrast to both the Brazilian and the Italian climates. Of course, the air was clogged with the fog of pollution from the steel mills. Objections to the polluted air were noted in private family gatherings but because working industry meant jobs for immigrants, not much was said publicly. Women adapted by hanging clean wash early Monday morning before the first and heaviest plumes of dirt came from the mills as they restarted. When mill whistles blew, women would rush to grab their damp wash from outside clothes lines and bring it inside to be hung on the backs of chairs and make-shift clothes lines strung across the kitchen.

It was now April 26th and a bed was set up for Giuseppe in an alcove off the kitchen in Rizzo's apartment at #3 Meadow Street. Newly arrived immigrants continued to be welcomed and occupied small living quarters shared by as many as three families in a house divided into three apartments. Connections to secure employment continued to be used, as well. In 1903 the economy was pretty good. There were many job choices in Pittsburgh giving Giuseppe the opportunity to choose where he wanted to work. Working for the railroad at that time was not an option. There was a general railroad strike in progress to protest against the anti-strike laws written with the political influence of industry owners on April 6th, just 20 days before Giuseppe arrived in America. Giuseppe would work for the railroad in later years as a coal stoker on steam trains. It was not a good time to start working in the steel mills. Unions had been eliminated by Andrew Carnegie through his mill manager Henry Frick, who boosted production by expanding work shifts to 12-hours and the standard work week to 6-days. Safety regulations were non-existent and pure exhaustion on the part of the workers made the job life-threatening.

Giuseppe's knowledge of agriculture, planting and harvesting coffee beans, and olive tree farming and olive oil production in Filogaso, made it natural for him to seek employment as a laborer in the gardens of Highland Park. By 1903, Highland Park was in the throes of grooming its 380 acres. Already established was the magnificent entrance graced by groomed gardens and a multi-tiered water fountain. There was no easy inroad for Giuseppe to use to network with the management of Highland Park because no one in the family worked there. Rizzo started making inquiries of others in the village until he learned of a friend of a friend who worked for the Park. The friend of a friend made the connection for Giuseppe. However, landing the job would be by his own wit. His timing was right. It was late spring and the early blooms were poking through remaining winter debris. During the interview, many words were not necessary as Giuseppe put his hands in the soil, sifting it through his fingers and making a trough around a budding hyacinth to demonstrate his expertise. Mr. Panzini, the grounds foreman, pursed his lips in a slight smile and offered Giuseppe a job. The starting wage for a laborer was about $53 a month. At the end of a 6-day-work-week, Giuseppe was paid $13.25. He was happy for the wage and was proud his work was on display in the beautiful gardens during the customary neighborhood Sunday strolls in the park. He would save what was left of his wage after contributing for his food and board at Giuseppe Rizzo's house. He needed $30 for Catarina's passage and $15 for Victoria's passage from the port at Naples to America, in addition to the required money she had to have with her to get through Ellis Island. He also needed passage money for himself to sail to Italy to escort her and Victoria to America, and money for travel to and from the Larimer Avenue Village to New York. In addition, he would need money to provide a living space for his family of three in America. As Giuseppe earned money in

47

America from his Highland Park job, he also earned money from odd jobs he picked up along the way. He was influenced by the way people became rich in America when he read about the new and innovative ways things were being done. The job he secured in America was to provide a living wage while he plotted his next move. He possessed years of experience with the Gallippi families' ventures in brokerage and his family-owned olive tree orchards and production of olive oil. Unlike other immigrants who were content making a living through an established American company job, Giuseppe concluded money could be made from more than one source.

By the middle of 1905, Giuseppe was ready to initiate a plan he had set up to go into business for himself. His plan was to arrange for the purchase of olives and olive oil made by growers around Filogaso for importing to America. It was clear there was a demand by grocers on both Larimer Avenue and Frankstown Road for Italian grown olives and authentic made olive oil for the thousands of Italian immigrants who settled in Pittsburgh. He had a *"Casaforta"* or a safe deposit box in the post office in Filogaso where his money was kept as there was no bank in the town. From this *"Casaforta"* came the funds through which Giuseppe's olive oil importing business started and continued to operate. The relationship Giuseppe had with Maria Catarina's brother Antonio Teti was one of trust. Through Antonio, connections for the business were made by Giuseppe when he planned to return to Filogaso. In February of 1905, the 29-year-old, Giuseppe boarded a steamship to Naples to see his wife and daughter, and to finish the arrangements for his new business.

Reunited

Giuseppe and Maria Catarina were like strangers to each other after being apart for over five years. Victoria did not know her father. She was shy and unsure until Giuseppe made special efforts to comfort her and find opportunities for her to get to know him. It was common then for Italian men to be away from their families for years at a time and for their children to have to adapt to them each time they returned. The wives of many Italian men were known to show off a little due to the money sent home from jobs in America.

All accounts show this was not the case for Maria Catarina. Her personality didn't lend itself to this sort of exhibitionism. When Maria Catarina's brother Antonio Teti, age 21, learned of Giuseppe's pending arrival he decided he wanted to come to America and began the process to obtain the proper passage papers so he could return with Giuseppe.

Giuseppe, Catarina and Victoria had only a month together before Giuseppe and Antonio Teti boarded the steamship the *"SS Weimer"* on March 16, 1905 from Naples for America. Giuseppe had all the arrangements for his successful import business in place. Fortunately, Giuseppe had been allowed to leave his job at Highland Park during the harsh winter months in Pittsburgh when there was little to do at the Park. He had to return by the beginning of April to his spring preparation duties.

The *"SS Weimer"* arrived in New York on March 31, 1905. Giuseppe Gallippi stayed with Antonio Teti as he was processed at Ellis Island. Antonio's last name was misspelled as *'Tete'*, a frequent occurrence for immigrants at that time. The two were greeted by friends Dominico Barbuto and Francesco La Piano in the **'Kissing Room'** before boarding the **'Train Ferry'** to Hoboken for the train ride to Pittsburgh.

S.S. WEIMAR, 1891 North German Lloyd
Courtesy The Peabody Museum of Salem

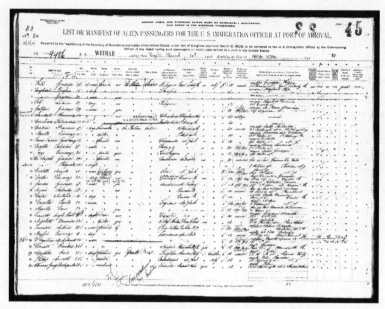

"SS Weimer" Manifest showing both Giuseppe Gallippi and Antonio Teti's names, #4 and #5, respectively. Details not easily read say Antonio was 21 years old, single, could not read or write and had $12. Giuseppe is listed as 29 years old, married, could read and write, had been in Pittsburgh for 3 years, and had $25. Both men were sponsored by Cousins Domenico Barbuto, 313 Everett Street, and Francesco LaPiana, 537 Highidon (Highland) Street. Neither had been in prison, neither was a polygamist or an anarchist. Each was in good mental and physical health and neither was deformed in any way.

While the train ride was long it seemed to pass quickly. Joining the group was none other than Giuseppe Rizzo and Raffaello Pizzo who sponsored another passenger, Giuseppe Tiso, a 26-year-old paesan farmer from Filogaso traveling to America on the same steamship. There was much conversation, laughter and discussion about the possibilities of work in America. A small welcoming party prepared by family and friends was ready for the group as they arrived in the Larimer Avenue village. Giuseppe was a happy man looking forward to a bright future.

NOTE: An important artifact of Giuseppe's was provided by his grandson Joseph Gallippi for this family story. Joe discovered an old *"F. Missler Bremen Steamship Emigrant Ticket and Document Wallet"* when looking through his father Vincenzo's *(known to our generation as Jimmy Gallippi)* items after his death. The wallet was used to carry Giuseppe's steamship tickets throughout his travels from Naples, Italy to Brazil; from San Paulo, Brazil to America; from America to Naples and Filogaso, Italy to reunite with Catarina and Victoria; on the return trip to America, and, finally to and from Naples and Filogaso to escort Catarina and Victoria to America. The pouch is pictured below and has a tale of its own.

Giuseppe's Ticket and Document Wallet

The ticket and document wallet measuring 8 1/2" by 7 1/8" is made of linen. These were given to emigrants by the biggest ticket agent around the turn of the century, Freidrich Missler, 30 Bahnhofstrasse, Bremen, Germany. The ship pictured on the front of the wallet *"The F. Missler"* is fictitious. No steamship of that name existed. However, the image has caused confusion by those who have been tracing their genealogy for decades by looking for the ***"SS Missler"*** only to find out Missler was the shipping line agent. Apparently he had established a solid working arrangement with the North German Lloyd Steamship Line and became wealthy due to the volume of steamship traffic by German-owned shipping companies during the height of emigration.

CHAPTER 3

VOYAGER MARIA CATARINA TETI GALLIPPI
(April 13, 1879 – July 23, 1951)

Background- Maria Catarina Teti Gallippi, the Teti Family

NOTE: The following information was graciously provided by cousin Tony Teti who lives in Etobicoke, Ontario, Canada just outside the city of Toronto. He lives with his wife Tina, near their three children and seven grandchildren. Tony is the grandson of Maria Catarina's brother Antonio. Without his generous sharing of information, our family would not have known the lineage of our Grandma Maria Catarina Teti's or our Grandpa Giuseppe Gallippi's families.

Before beginning Maria Catarina's story, I want to salute Giuseppe. He had such an adventurous life, and his stories would have mesmerized us as children had we had the opportunity to hear them from his lips. He lived in Brazil, traveling across the Atlantic Ocean many times and was not afraid to take risks to earn money for his family. He and our family displayed their generosity to their fellow countrymen and women as needs arose. He anchored the Gallippi family in the Larimer Avenue Village, laying the groundwork from which our opportunities came. It is sad to think that only two of my generation as very young children knew him because he died in 1929 before most of us were born.

As young children we knew our Grandma Gallippi, who preferred her friends and extended family call her Catarina. We called her Nonni. After she emigrated from Italy in 1906, she lived in the Larimer Avenue Village until she died on July 23, 1951 at the age of 72.

She was a fixture in our family. She had long white hair that she twisted around her fingers before wrapping it in a bun she secured with hairpins at the back of her head. A soft wave in her hair framed her face and she wore patterned cotton house dresses.

Catherine Gallippi in 1945

Catarina grew vegetables and flowers in her garden and peach trees grew on the terraced hillside behind her home. She made tasty homemade pastas and breads. There was always a pot of hot soup on the stove in her kitchen for whoever came in the front door. You could count on it.

Stories of her personal generosity and strength, and the activity in and around her home at 529 Lenora Street, are legend. Her large kitchen was the gathering place for the family.

Catarina Teti's Family

Catarina's family has deep roots in Filogaso Italy, dating back to the 1700's. Catarina was the great, great, great, granddaughter of **Domenico Teti & Caterina Urso.** Her great, great grandparents were **Antonio Teti and Lucrezia Borgia Teti.** Antonio and Lucrezia had five children. **Francesco,** the oldest, married and lived in the Teti family home in Filogaso. *(For five years, when Giuseppe was working in Brazil and then in America, his wife Catarina and his* *daughter Victoria lived in that home with Francesco and his wife.)* **Domenico,** the second son, may have been the conduit through which the Gallippi and Teti families learned of the Larimer Avenue community and the work available in Pittsburgh in the 1800's. **Giuseppe,** the third son, married and had two children named **Antonio** and **Maria. Vincenzo, the fourth son, was our Great Grandfather. He married our Great Grandmother Vittoria Tarascio.** The fifth and final child born to Antonio and Lucrezia Borgia was **Caterina,** the only girl. Caterina lived to be 100 years old and was the only woman in Filogaso who owned a Singer Sewing Machine. She sewed many garments for the community while she lived in her home in Filogaso with her 20 cats. *(See the Teti family tree on pages 64,65,66)*

Our Great Grandparents **Vincenzo Teti** and **Victoria Tarascio** Teti had three children. They were **Lucrezia** *(1876-1947);* **Maria Catarina** (our Grandmother) *(1879-1951),* and **Antonio** *(1884-1913).* Catarina's older sister **Lucrezia** was married at 13-years old in an arranged marriage to her cousin **Vincenzo Teti**. Family memories indicate she was so frightened at the prospect of being married to a man she barely knew, that she ran away on her wedding day creating a flurry of activity until she was found and coaxed back home. Apparently the coaxing worked because she

Maria Catarina was born in this house

Great Aunt Lucrezia and Uncle Vincenzo

gave birth to six children. Family stories relate that her oldest son **Francesco** emigrated to America in 1913, got into trouble with some unsavory characters, was harmed in a knife fight, disappeared and was never heard from again. **Domenico** immigrated to Argentina and also got in with a "bad" crowd, disappeared and died early in his life in Argentina. **Vincenzo** stayed in Filogaso. **Lucrezia** emigrated to Argentina and has a daughter **Gelormina. Giuseppe,** emigrated to Argentina, worked as a laborer and married **Caterina,** an Argentinian woman. After several years, he left Caterina in Argentina and returned to Italy bringing with him grape vines to help replenish those that were destroyed by disease, and olive trees to plant in Filogaso. He then married **Theresa Tarascio** and had two children, **Lucrezia** and **Caterina.** The youngest son **Antonio** stayed in Filogaso, married **Francesca Nano** and had 10 children. They were **Vincenzo,** who lives in Toronto, Canada with his wife; **Francesco; Lucrezia,** who lives in Toronto, Canada; **Giuseppe; Domenico,** who lives in Toronto with his wife **Paola; Crescenza, Carmelo, Caterina, Immacolata** and **Pasquala,** who all live in Italy.

(Pictured below are Lucrezia's son Antonio's children who live in Toronto I met for the first time during my 2014 visit Toronto to gather information on our family. They were as anxious to meet me as I was to meet them and share our families' connections.)

Vincenzo & Wife

Domenico, Paola & Lucrezia

Great Uncle Antonio in late 1800's

Great Aunt Rosa Teti

Francesco Teti as a soldier in WWII in the 1940's

Grandma Catarina's younger brother **Great Uncle Antonio** traveled to America from Italy on the steamship the *"S.S. Weimar"*. He was with Giuseppe, our Grandpa, who was returning from Filogaso to America after being reunited with his family after five years. The pair left from the Port in Naples on March 16, 1905 arriving at Ellis Island on March 31, 1905. Great Uncle Antonio eventually returned to live in Filogaso. He married **Rosa Teti** in 1908 and had two children. They were **Vincenzo,** who died at 17-years-old in September of 1924, and **Francesco,** *(1849-1976).* Francesco was adventurous. He travelled to Africa, Portugal and ultimately to Pittsburgh, PA. Family stories tell of his bringing back to Filogaso olive trees from Africa, and olive and orange trees from Portugal. He married **Maria Mari** and they had two children, **Rosa,** who at this writing is 79 and lives in Filogaso, and **Antonio (Tony) Teti,** 77, who lives in Etobicoke, Ontario Canada near Toronto. Rosa married and had three children - **Domenico, Victoria** and **Maria.**

Her daughter Victoria became a lawyer and died at age 50 much to the heartbreak of the family. Antonio (Tony) Teti married **Agatha (Tina) DeCaria** and emigrated to Toronto, Canada in 1956. They currently reside in Etobicoke, Ontario near Toronto and have three children – **Francesco, John** and **Maria;** and seven grandchildren – **Olivia, Lucas, Dylan, Anthony, Ava, Atina** and **Emma.** Although Tony worked as a tailor after he emigrated to Canada, his first love was and still is music. He plays the clarinet and was a member of a marching band in Filogaso.

Pictures of the Antonio Teti family below, courtesy of Tony Teti

Tony Teti's mother Maria visiting her sisters
and niece at their home in Argentina

A young Tony Teti in his band uniform in Italy

A mature Tony & Tina Teti, and their children
Francesco, John & Maria, in a recent picture

Picture taken in 1936 of Tony's sister Rosa with
a family member in Filogaso, Italy

Maria and Francesco Teti

Connection to Filogaso, Italy Continues

Today, Tony Teti owns the original Teti family home in Filogaso, Italy, that is located on *"Via Roma"*, the main street of the town. Since he took ownership, he and Tina have renovated the home which is the same home that our Nonni Catarina and Aunt Victoria lived in while Grandpa Giuseppe worked in San Paulo, Brazil. The Teti family returns to the family home as often as possible. They maintain the language and cultural traditions of Filogaso in Toronto and encourage their children and grandchildren to do the same. Tina grows a garden filled with the family's favorite foods. Every day she makes fresh pasta, and prepares meals for her family from what she has grown in her garden. The family makes its own sausage and involves the whole family in caning enough tomatoes for everyone to use throughout the year. Some of their wines are homemade, particularly a sweet white that enhances whatever else is being served. Other wines are custom-made from a variety of grapes grown and bottled in the wineries along Lake Ontario near Toronto. Tony and Tina stay engaged with their children and grandchildren daily, frequently eating dinner together.

Today, there are 600,000 Italians living in Toronto...a significant cultural force. It might seem strange to refer to this portion of Canada as an expanded village of Italians; but, culturally around the Toronto area it is just that as traditions and holidays are shared. Every member of the family and their friends are welcomed and embraced no matter if they have spent their lives together or have found each other after a lifetime apart.

This Toronto community maintains its connection to Italy. Every Wednesday, there is a direct air flight from the *"Lester B. Pearson International Airport"* near Tony's home to the *"Lamezia Terme Airport"* in southern Italy near Filogaso.

Welcome

We are all in this together — and we are glad you are visiting our site. This is our online meeting place, where we organize our activities, share ideas, and publicize our mission.

Our Mission

We work together to celebrate our ancestry and traditions. Our wish is to reach out to those who share our vision. Whether you're ready to lend a hand at one of our activities, participate in our events or have ideas you would like to share, we'd like to hear from you. Go to the "Contact Us" page to submit ideas or ask questions.

Feast

of the
Madonna del Carmine
Sunday July 21, 2013

Mass - 10:30 a.m.
Picnic - 1:00 p.m.
Magic Show - 1:30 p.m.
Games - 3:00 p.m.

Teti Family Tree -- Maria Catarina Teti Gallippi

Domenico Teti & Caterina Urso -- (Great, Great, Great, Great, Great Grandparents)
(No Birth Records- were destroyed in the Earthquake of 1800)

(Great, Great, Great Grandparents)
Vincenzo Teti + Victoria Lovento
(Born 1799)

(Great, Great Grandparents)
Antonio Teti + Lucrezia Borgia Teti
(Born 1818)   (Born 1825)

(Great, Grandparents)

Vincenzo married **Vittoria Tarascio**   **Victoria**   **Caterina**
(Born 1847) / (Born 1-9-1884)   (1855-1861)   (Born 1857)
single, lived to
100 had 20 cats.

(Grandparents)

Francesco + Giovanna Consentino   **Domenico**+Maddaline Teti
(Born 1849)   (Born 1859)

Antonio, Victoria, Scangiaferrra   Lucrezia, Caterina, Victoria, Antonio

Giuseppe + Maria Gallippi
(1852-1932)/

Rachele Arena, Vincenzo

Giuseppe, Angela - (Antonio, Rachele, Constantia)

Maria Catarina married **Giuseppe Gallippi**
(1879-1951)
(Giuseppe to Brazil then with Catarina to US)

Great Uncle **Antonio** married **Rosa Teti**
(Born 1884) /
Vincenzo,   Francesco
died at 17   / went
Sept. 15, 1924   to Africa, in
African Army
brought back
olive trees to Filogaso

Virginia   Benedetto   Emilio   Adalina
Jan 11, 1915   Oct 5, 1916   Dec 16, 1918   Jan 14, 1920
2009   1999   2001   2001

Rosalia   Almina
Jan 25, 1911   Apr 18, 1913
2011   2008

Great Aunt **Lucrezia** married **Vincenzo Teti**
(1876-1947) /

Francesco, Dominico, Giuseppe, Antonio, Vincenzo Lucrezia

America   Argentina   Filogaso Argentina
1913

Grandaughter lives in Filogaso

Antonina   Antonio   Vincenzo
Dec 6, 1906   May 26, 1908   Nov 1, 1909
1981   1987   1991

Doris
(1943)

Victoria
Feb 6, 1900
1985

Janet
(1938)

Rosanne   Carolyn   Nancy
(1956)   (1968)   (1971)

Linda
(1967)

Chelsea   Riley   Katie, Nina   Taylor   Quinn
(2003)   (2003)   (2002)   (2004)   (2007)

Gillian
(2000)

64

Teti Family Tree -- Maria Catarina Teti Gallippi (continued)

(Great, Great, Great Grandparents)
Vincenzo Teti + Victoria Lovento
(Born 1799)

(Great, Great Grandparents)
Antonio Teti + Lucrezia Borgia Teti
6 children

(Great Grandparents)

Francesco	Domenico	Giuseppe	**Vincenzo-married Vittoria Tarascio**	**Caterina**	**Victoria**
				lived to be 100/only Singer	
				Sewing Machine in village/ had 20 cats	

Maria Catarina Teti -married Giuseppe Gallippi   *Antonio Teti - married Rosa Teti*

(Great Aunt) **Lucrezia Teti - married Vincenzo Teti**
(Married at 13 years old)

Francesco	Dominico	Giuseppe	Antonio	Vincenzo	Lucrezia
Went to America in 1913. Got into trouble and was injured in a knifing. Disappeared (No picture)	Went to Argentina. Did not get along with the family. Got in with a bad crowd. Disappeared. Died thereafter.	Laborer. Planted fruit and olives. Went to Argentina. While there married **Caterina**. Came back to Filogaso, married Teresa Tarascio and had 2 children... **Lucrezia** and **Caterina**.	Lived in Filogaso. Married **Francesca Nano**. Had 10 children. **Vincenzo** lives in Toronto, Canada; **Francesco; Lucrezia** lives in Toronto; **Giuseppe; Domenico** married **Paola** & lives in Toronto & in Filogaso are **Crescenza, Carmelo,Immacolata, Caterina & Pasquala**	Living in Argentina.	Went to Argentina, married and has 2 children... a boy and a girl who live in Argentina.

65

Teti Family Tree – Maria Catarina Teti Gallippi (continued)

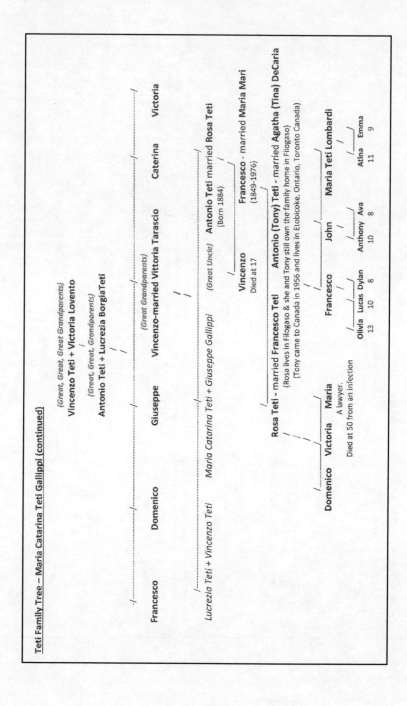

(Great, Great, Great Grandparents)
Vincenzo Teti + Victoria Lovento

(Great, Great, Grandparents)
Antonio Teti + Lucrezia Borgia Teti

(Great Grandparents)

Francesco   Domenico   Giuseppe   Vincenzo–married Vittoria Tarascio   Caterina   Victoria

Lucrezia Teti + Vincenzo Teti   *Maria Catarina Teti + Giuseppe Gallippi*   *(Great Uncle)*   **Antonio Teti married Rosa Teti**
(Born 1884)

Vincenzo   Francesco - married Maria Mari
Died at 17   (1849-1976)

Rosa Teti - married Francesco Teti   Antonio (Tony) Teti - married Agatha (Tina) DeCaria
(Rosa lives in Filogaso & she and Tony still own the family home in Filogaso)
(Tony came to Canada in 1956 and lives in Etobicoke, Ontario, Toronto Canada)

Domenico   Victoria   Maria   Francesca   John   Maria Teti Lombardi
A lawyer.
Died at 50 from an infection

Olivia   Lucas   Dylan   Anthony   Ava   Atina   Emma
  13   10   8   10   8   11   9

The Story of Maria Catarina Coming to America

By the early 1900's, immigrant men who had settled in America were ready to bring their wives and children to join them, instead of sailing to and from their home countries to see them. Giuseppe Gallippi and Giuseppe Rizzo began planning to bring their wives and children to America. For Giuseppe it would be one more year before Catarina and Victoria could join the cascade of Italian immigrants filling the Larimer Avenue Village. It was a time of challenges for him as he worked at earning extra money for his passage so he could accompany them on their voyage to America. Not all of his business efforts were successful; but, he eventually earned the money he needed. Rizzo, who had lived in America longer than Giuseppe, not only earned enough money to bring his wife Concette Gallippi to America, he earned enough to purchase a house on Orphan Street in which he planned to raise a family. Rizzo's plan meant there would be more room in the Meadow Street house for Giuseppe's family. Before leaving for Italy, Giuseppe rented two floors of the home to be sure there would be a place for his family to live. Catarina and Giuseppe's additional nine children were born at 3 Meadow Street.

Catarina's Voyage to America in 1906.

The time had come. In January of 1906, Giuseppe traveled across the bitterly cold Atlantic Ocean to the warmth of Naples, and then to Filogaso to prepare Catarina for her voyage to America. On March 7, 1906, Giuseppe escorted his wife Catarina and 6-year-old Victoria Gallippi to America on the steamship *"SS Konigin Luise"*. Traveling with them were Concette Gallippi Rizzo, wife of Giuseppe Rizzo, and another Gallippi cousin, Domenic Gallippi.

Catarina was apprehensive. She was leaving her village, the only home she had known. Although she had heard favorable stories from her Uncle Domenic Teti and others who had gone before her, America still was the great unknown to Catarina where a different language would be spoken and traditions would not be those to which she was accustomed. Like other women in Italy of her time, Catarina was not taught to read or write as her duties were to keep the home and feed the family. However, Catarina was a strong, smart woman who became more of a partner to Giuseppe. She trusted him to do right by her and felt being with him was far better than being without him. Giuseppe valued their partnership, and there are family stories of how they worked well together and had genuine affection for one another.

It was said to be a good marriage welcomed by both of them. With all arrangements made for Catarina's and Victoria's passage, the three Gallippi's and their cousins boarded the steamship *"SS Konigin Luise"* in Naples, Italy on the cloudy, moonless night of February 23, in the leap year of 1906.

The bitter cold and shortened days of winter keep most steerage passengers below, wrapped in their warm, homespun wool capes. For Catarina, it was a special time. She was reunited with her husband who, on his sixth steamship voyage, used his experience to reassure her throughout the long trip across the Atlantic Ocean. They talked of his plans, of the gardens they would plant and the freedom he had enjoyed in the company of other Italians in the Larimer Avenue Village. And when they weren't talking, Victoria provided a source of enjoyment. Her bright-eyed curiosity and imagination amused other passengers. She played with the one toy she was allowed to bring which was a homemade brown bear with very long arms, crocheted eyes, nose and upturned mouth that always smiled at her. The bear wore an onion-skin-died muslin dress with a red, ribbon-like waistband, and a matching triangle scarf on its head. Victoria had named her bear Philomena. When Victoria played with other children on the ship she put Philomena on her mama's lap for safe-keeping.

The *"SS Konigin Luise"* arrived in New York at Ellis Island 13 days later on March 7, 1906 as the sky brightened with the light of the nearly full moon. Passengers were awakened to the shouts of crew members and the jolt of dropping the anchor. As they were in the belly of the ship no one could see the action or the Statue of Liberty. They were told to gather their belongings and to prepare to walk down the long plank to the barge that would take them to Ellis. At first, most were too weary and groggy to be emotional at arriving in America.

However, as the sun broke through in the early hours, energy returned. The Statue was visible in the morning light; and, there was no objection to the greeting cold breeze. They had arrived at the port of their new lives.

Processing immigrants at Ellis had not changed since Giuseppe made his first voyage to America. Catarina and Victoria were processed as were others and, before long, Giuseppe, Catarina, Concetta, Dominic, Victoria and Philomena were on the **'Train Ferry'** to Hoboken to complete the journey to their new home.

Notes marked on the back of this old envelope were the only family records of Catarina, Giuseppe & Victoria's travels to America in 1906. These clues led to the development of the story of their relocation to America.

Arrival at the Larimer Avenue Village

It was the noise that first grabbed Catarina's attention as they disembarked from the train. There was so much of it. The air was dirty and so clogged with soot that the sun could barely be seen through the haze. Only a few shards of light marked her path as the group walked along Liberty Avenue to board the streetcar bound for Larimer Avenue and #3 Meadow Street. Catarina kept looking for bright colors; but, everything around her was brown, even the snow piles along the streets. There was no color. She started to have doubts as Filogaso was clean and green, warm and quiet. She shook her head at knowing there would be many adjustments to make.

The Meadow Street apartment was the first clean thing she had seen since arriving in America. Giuseppe turned on the gas heater to warm the rooms and lit the lanterns for Catarina to see her new home. It had two large bedrooms and a kitchen large enough to hold a couch and an overstuffed chair in addition to the sink, icebox, stove, table and four chairs.

She noted the apartment had a few wide windows and there was a washroom; but, no 'pishadoo' *(southern Italian slang for toilet)*. She was expecting to see one from the rumors she heard about America. Giuseppe explained that everyone would have a pishadoo soon; but, for now, it was the *'backhouse' (outhouse)* which wasn't much different from the way it was in Filogaso, except it was colder. The good thing was the apartment was on ground level and she could walk into the back yard or on the street without any trouble. And, there was a dirt-floor cellar, ideal for storing food and other supplies. As the apartment warmed, Catarina imagined the garden she would plant and liked the idea that Victoria could play outside within eyesight.

Word of Catarina's arrival spread quickly in the village among the many friends Giuseppe made in his three years in America. The welcoming started when Giuseppe Rizzo, Concette, Dominic, and other family members arrived.

Rizzo's booming voice rang out "Giuseppe, Giuseppe, open the door!" In marched Rizzo with the group that included cousin Alimina, holding a cast iron pot filled with hot chicken soup; along with her husband Guillermo and their three children, Vincenzo, Antonio and five-year-old Carmella holding her dolly Maria. Ten-year-old Vincenzo presented eight small loaves of freshly made Easter Bread to Catarina.

Seven-year-old Antonio, shyly presented her with a wedge of cheese. Rizzo had his own surprise... a bottle of vino from his homemade stock. Catarina's eyes teared up as Alimina put the pot of soup on the stove and pulled out a tablecloth, napkins, small bowls,a large soup ladle plus spoons, forks and a knife from her satchel as she was not sure what was in the apartment. Giuseppe quickly reached in the cupboard for some dishes and wine glasses he had purchased a few months after he arrived in America. He called for Catarina and everyone else to sit at the table.

Everyone was hungry and the feast began in earnest. No sooner was the main course finished; the front door opened and in came other village neighbors carrying small gifts for Catarina and Dominic's wife Concette to help them get settled.

Small paper bags contained homemade cookies, embroidered pillow cases, an apron, a serving dish, odd bowls and plates, and cups and saucers. Whatever strangeness Catarina felt about her new home left her for a while as she was surrounded by laughter, gifts, welcoming hugs and people speaking in a language she understood. The hum of conversation, punctuated by an occasional song, filled the room as Carmella and Maria played with Victoria and Philomena.

When the sun began to set, neighbors said their goodbyes with as much energy as they had coming in. Alimina left with a promise to show Catarina and Concette where the shops were around the village the next day. Before departing to their home on Orphan Street, Rizzo spoke briefly of work as Giuseppe was anxious to get back to work at Highland Park the next day. He had spent much money getting his family to America and needed to earn more.

Catarina never forgot the kindness and generosity extended to her; and, stories of her generosity throughout her life in America are legend. She would share whatever she could with others many times.

A Marriage for Victoria

In 1913, the very beautiful, olive-eyed Victoria was 13-years-old. Giuseppe arranged a marriage for her with Nicola Martino, a swarthy Italian man more than 10 years her senior. Family members' recollections are that Nicola was living in Italy at the time and was sent for with sponsorship arranged by Giuseppe. However, when searching for Nicola's immigration records, dozens of men with that name were listed and without any other information about him, distinguishing one from another was nearly impossible.

When Victoria and Nicola set eyes on each other, they liked what they saw and the courting began in earnest. There was so much earnest, in fact, that the two were seen kissing on the front stoop of the house by Catarina, and about a dozen other neighbors who were quick to share the news. There was an uproar! It was strictly taboo for unmarried couples to kiss and to do so in public was thought to bring shame to the family. Catarina and Giuseppe insisted the two "had" to be married and married quickly.

As a result, a family member was dispatched to Our Lady Help of Christian Church to consult a priest and arrange for a speedy marriage to save the family name. They were married the following week. It is said Victoria was a beautiful bride.

By the time Victoria married, five more children were born to Catarina and Giuseppe. Antonina (Ann), born December 6, 1906; Antonio (Tony), born May 26, 1908; Vincenzo (Jimmy), born November 1, 1909; Rosalia Anna (Rose), born January 25, 1911; and Alimina (Mimi), born April 18, 1913. The older children slept upstairs in the converted 2nd floor apartment rooms made into bedrooms in the very full home.

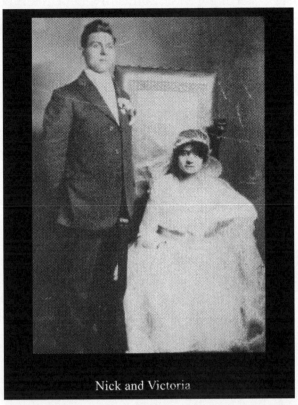
Nick and Victoria

13-year-old Victoria & Nicola Martino on their wedding day

The years from 1913 to 1915 were filled with vibrant family activity. At that time America was expanding its communications capabilities. The Gallippi family heard radio station KDKA musical broadcasts in the evenings from the floor-model, mahogany radio in the back of the kitchen near the daybed. In 1913, theaters began to open in East Liberty each with a stage large enough to accommodate live performances and eventually movies. The *'Bijou Dream Nickelodeon'* was the first, followed by the *'Cameraphone'*, *'Regent'*, *'Liberty'*, *'Empire'*, *'Triangle'*, *'Haltis'* and lastly, the *'Sheridan Square'*.[81] A short streetcar ride from the Larimer Avenue Village allowed access to performances by East Liberty native musicians Billy Strayhorn, Erroll Garner, Billy Eckstine and Mary Lou Williams; and performances by Dick Powell, Gene Kelly and his brother Fred Kelly. Movies became a hit attraction when **'My**

Man Godfrey', starring Carole Lombard and William Powell; and *'Mistress Nell'*, starring Mary Pickford were featured. Of course, the children were too young to actually attend any of these performances. It's reasonable to assume Antonina, Tony, Rose, Jimmy and Mimi overheard their excited aunts and uncles discussing the changes in their community during those customary Sunday afternoon family gatherings.

Hard work was the order of the weekday. Giuseppe continually sought several sources of income through those years. He maintained his job at Highland Park, worked his carpentry skills for side money; and according to census records, opened a grocery store in 1915, that he and Catarina ran from their Meadow Street front porch just off the corner of busy Larimer Avenue. The store featured home grown vegetables from their property, and olives and olive oil products. From 1915 to 1920, the couple's last four children were born. They were Virginia - January 11, 1915; Benedetto - October 5, 1916; Emilio - December 16, 1918; and Adalina Carmella - January 14, 1920. The January 8, 1920 census listed Giuseppe as a Laborer for a paper company.

```
      blug
Galliott Harry carp 5143 Holmes
Gallippi Jos grocer 3 Meadow
Gallis Mary wid Albert 2100 S 18th
Gallisath Jos jeweler 525 Gross
Gallisheh Julia wid Wm 2707½ Carey ay
Gallius Jos lab 802 Shelby
Gallmus Philip 56 Excelsior
Gallnot C P mgr Baum boul and Beatty S
    h 6953 Bennett
Gallnot Camille slsmn 417½ Beatty N
Gallo Frank lab 70 Graphic
Gallo Hanibal bartndr 701 Wylie av
Gallo Michl barber 602 Preble av
Gallo Michl lab 57 Congress
Gallo Philip M dftsmn 362 La Marido
Gallon Andw lunchrm 6335 Frankstown av
    h 543 Turrett
Galloney Lewis lab 506 Reliance E
Gallovits John lab 104 Climax
Gallovits Louis lab 104 Climax
Gallovits Wm 104 Climax
Gallow Chas lab 469 Taylor
```

Pittsburgh 1915 Census listing Joe Gallippi as Grocer

74

In 1922, Giuseppe secured a well-paying job with the Pennsylvania Railroad in Pittsburgh as a coal stoker on steam trains. It was a job he held until his death on June 25, 1929.

Also in 1922, the family, with the exception of Victoria, who was most probably naturalized through her marriage to Nicola, were recognized as naturalized American citizens even though nine of them were American citizens because they were born in America. Giuseppe wanted to be sure he, his wife and his children were "official Americans". By then they had grown roots in this country. The adult children would later joke that they were "Twice Americans", once by birth and once by naturalization.

U. S. DEPARTMENT OF LABOR
NATURALIZATION SERVICE

UNITED STATES OF AMERICA

OATH OF ALLEGIANCE

PETITION FOR NATURALIZATION

To the Honorable the District Court of the United States for the Western District of Pennsylvania:

The petition of .... **Giuseppe Gallippi** ....

First. My place of residence is .... **3 Meadow St., Pittsburgh** .... Pennsylvania.

Second. My occupation is .... **Laborer** ....

Third. I was born on the .... **29th** .... **September** .... anno domini **1875** at .... **Foglia Italy** ....

Fourth. I emigrated to the United States from .... **Santo Brasil** .... on or about the .... **10th** .... **April** .... I arrived in the United States, at the port of .... **Capre** .... on the .... **24th April** ....

Fifth. I declared my intention to become a citizen of the United States on the .... **27th** .... day of .... **April** .... anno domini **919** at .... **Pittsburgh** .... in the .... **District** .... Court of .... **United States** ....

Sixth. I am .... **married**. My wife's name is .... **Catherine** .... she was born in .... **Italy** .... and now resides at .... **withme** ....

I have **10** children, and the name, date and place of birth, and place of residence of each of said children is as follows:

Vittoria – Feb 6 1900 Italy, Pittsburgh Virginia Jan 11 1916 Pittsburgh Pittsburgh
Antonia – Dec 6 1905 Penna. " Benedetto – Oct 5 1916 " "
Assanio – May 25 1908 " " Emilio – Dec 16 19 " "
Vincenzo – Nov 1 1909 " " Adilina – Jan 14 1920 " "
Rosalia – Jan 25 1911 " "
Alminia – Apr 18 1913 " "

Seventh. I am not a disbeliever in or opposed to organized government or a member of or affiliated with any organization or body of persons teaching disbelief in or opposed to organized government. I am not a polygamist nor a believer in the practice of polygamy. I am attached to the principles of the Constitution of the United States, and it is my intention to become a citizen of the United States and to renounce absolutely and forever all allegiance and fidelity to any foreign prince, potentate, state, or sovereignty, and particularly to .... **VICTOR EMMANUEL III, KING OF ITALY** .... of whom at this time I am a subject, and it is my intention to reside permanently in the United States.

Eighth. I am able to speak the English language.

Ninth. I have resided continuously in the United States of America for the term of five years at least, immediately preceding the date of this petition, to wit, since the .... **24th** .... day of .... **April** .... anno domini **903** and in the State of Pennsylvania, continuously next preceding the date of this petition, since the .... **25th** .... day of .... **April** .... anno domini **903** being a residence within this State of at least one year next preceding the date of this petition.

Tenth. I have not heretofore made petition for citizenship to any court. I made petition for citizenship to the .... **United States District** .... Court of .... **U.S.** .... at .... **Pittsburgh Pa.** .... on the .... **15th** .... day of .... **February** .... anno domini **911** the said petition was denied by the said Court for the following reasons and causes, to wit: .... **Said Petition No 4478 Was dismissed** .... **"Fail to Prosecute"** .... and the cause of such denial has since been cured or removed.)

Attached hereto and made a part of this petition are my declaration of intention to become a citizen of the United States and the certificate from the Department of Labor, together with my affidavit and the affidavits of the two verifying witnesses thereto, required by law. Wherefore your petitioner prays that he may be admitted a citizen of the United States of America.

Declaration of Intention No. **57510**, and Certificate of Arrival No. **XX XX** .... from Department of Labor filed this .... day of ....

NOTE TO CLERK OF COURT.—If petitioner arrived in the United States on or after June 29, 1906, strike out the words reading "and Certificate of Arrival No. .... from Department of Labor."

AFFIDAVITS OF PETITIONER AND WITNESSES

UNITED STATES OF AMERICA,
Western District of Pennsylvania.

The aforesaid petitioner being duly sworn, deposes and says that he is the petitioner in the above-entitled proceedings; that he has read the foregoing petition and knows the contents thereof; that the said petition is signed with his full, true name; that the same is true of his own knowledge except as to matters therein stated to be alleged upon information and belief, and that as to those matters he believes it to be true.

Giuseppe Rizzo .... Laborer .... Pittsburgh
Giuseppe Chiodo .... Shoemaker ....

each being severally, duly, and respectively sworn, deposes and says that he is a citizen of the United States of America; that he has personally known **Giuseppe Gallippi** .... the petitioner above mentioned, to have resided in the United States continuously immediately preceding the date of filing his petition, since the .... **1st** .... day of .... **January** .... anno domini **1917** and in the State of Pennsylvania continuously since the .... **1st** .... day of .... **January** .... anno domini **1917** and that he has personal knowledge that the said petitioner is a person of good moral character, attached to the principles of the Constitution of the United States, and that he is in every way qualified, in his opinion, to be admitted a citizen of the United States.

Subscribed and sworn to before me this .... **15th** .... day of ....

Petition for Naturalization

Jozef Kurzawski

OATH OF ALLEGIANCE

I hereby declare, on oath, that I absolutely and entirely renounce and abjure all allegiance and fidelity to any foreign prince, potentate, state, or sovereignty, and particularly to _____ the _____ of whom I have heretofore been a subject; that I will support and defend the Constitution and laws of the United States of America against all enemies, foreign and domestic; and that I will bear true faith and allegiance to the same.

Subscribed and sworn to before me, in op

NOTE.—

Upon consideration of the petition of

further testimony taken in open Court, it is ord

to become a citizen of the United States of Am

(It is further ordered, upon consideratio

and hereby is, changed to

June 29, 1906 (34 Stat. L., pt. 1, p. 596), as am

By the Court:

Upon consideration of the petition of

THE SAID PETITION IS HEREBY DENIE

Continued from

to

Continued from

Certificate of Naturalization, No. issued on the _____ day of _____ A. D. 19

2774

U. S. DEPARTMENT OF LABOR
NATURALIZATION SERVICE

No. 57510

TRIPLICATE

UNITED STATES OF AMERICA

DECLARATION OF INTENTION

☞ Invalid for all purposes seven years after the date hereof

State of Pennsylvania,
Western District of Pennsylvania, } ss:

In the District Court of the United Sta

I, G. Giuseppe Callippi, aged 43 year

occupation laborer, do declare on oath that my personal

description is: Color white, complexion dark, height feet, inche

weight 125 pounds, color of hair brown, color of eyes brown

other visible distinctive marks none

I was born in Polyo Italy

on the 7th day of September 875; I now resi

at 85 Monday St. Pittsburg Pennsylvani

I emigrated to the United States of America from Naples Santo Brazil

on the vessel Capre, my la

foreign residence was Polyga

of my wife is Catherine, I am married; the nam

and now resides at — with me she was born at — in Italy

It is my bona fide intention to renounce forever all allegiance and fidelity to any foreig

prince, potentate, state, or sovereignty, and particularly to

of whom I am now a subject

I arrived at the port of New York

State of New York on or about the 24th da

of April, anno Domini 1 905; I am not an anarchist; I am not a

polygamist nor a believer in the practice of polygamy; and it is my intention in good faith

to become a citizen of the United States of America and to permanently reside therein:

SO HELP ME GOD.

Giuseppe Callippi

[SEAL]

Subscribed and sworn to before me in the office of the Clerk of said Cour

at Pittsburgh, Pa., this 23rd day of April

anno Domini 191

J. W. Clark

Clerk of the District Court of the United Sta

By _____, Deputy Cler

Giuseppe's Declaration of Intention for Citizenship

Giuseppe's Certification of Naturalization

Antonina Marries Francesco Caschera

In 1920, when Antonina was 14-years-old, Giuseppe made arrangements with the Caschera family in Italy for their son Francesco to marry Catarina and Giuseppe's second daughter, the petite and raven-haired Antonina. Antonina and Francesco were married at Our Lady Help of Christian Church shortly after his arrival to the Larimer Avenue Village. The couple had two children, Antonina who died as an infant and Joseph who had a successful career in U.S. Government work. Joseph is 84 years old at this writing and lives in a comfortable retirement home near Dayton, Ohio.

A young Antonina Gallippi

Giuseppe Gallippi   Ann and Frank Caschera   Family friends of Frank

The marriage of Antonina Gallippi & Francesco Caschera

Antonina's marriage, like the arranged marriage of Victoria, did not go the way Catarina envisioned. There are older family stories of why those years were difficult that can't be verified at this writing because the principals died long ago. Only vague memories and secondhand information exists. It would be a disservice to either woman or their families to write anything not verifiable. We do know back in those days, it was the custom for the men to rule the family and dominate their wives. The fact that women were not even allowed to choose their husbands pretty much tells the story. We know Victoria became ill early in her marriage with Nicola, and both Nicola and Francesco made all the decisions for their wives and children. Over time Catarina became disenchanted with the idea of arranged marriages and abandoned that idea for the remainder of her daughters. She told them they were on their own to find their mates vowing there would be no more arranged marriages in her family... and, there were not.

Nicola and Victoria Buy Their First House

In April of 1924, Nicola and Victoria bought a large, three-story house at 569 Lenora Street that overlooked Washington Boulevard. By then two children had been born to the couple. Agnes was born on April 24, 1921 and Catherine (Kay), in 1923. It was not unlike Nicola to purchase property, as he bought and sold several properties. His goal, like many men of his time, was to become a rich man. Family verbal history indicates he succeeded after moving to California where he purchased prime properties in the late 1920's. Through an arrangement between Giuseppe and Nicola, Giuseppe and Catarina bought the house at 569 Lenora Street on August 19, 1924 for one dollar. Giuseppe then got a mortgage from the *"Liberty Building and Loan Association"* for $3,000 using the property as collateral. The loan was paid off less than three years later on May 25, 1927. There are no records giving clues about what they did with the money they borrowed or why the transaction was made that way. We can speculate some of it probably went to Nicola to use to buy more property, and some was used to purchase olives and olive oil from Italy to import to America for Giuseppe's business.

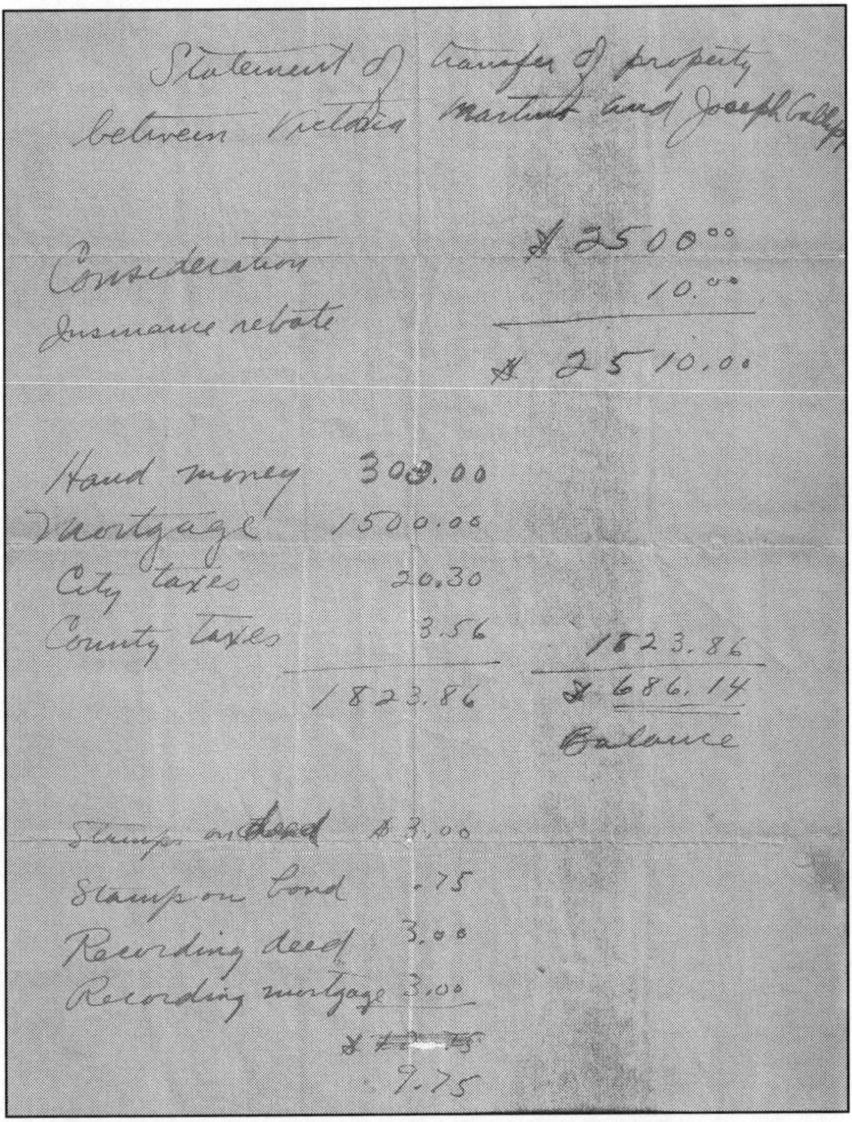

Statement of transfer of property
between Victoria Martino and Joseph Gallippi

Consideration $2500.00
Insurance rebate   10.00
                                 _____
                                 $ 2510.00

Hand money   300.00
Mortgage   1500.00
City taxes   20.30
County taxes   3.56   1823.86
                  _____ $ 686.14
                  1823.86   Balance

Stamps on deed $3.00
Stamp on bond   .75
Recording deed   3.00
Recording mortgage 3.00
                  $ ____
                  9.75

Initial unofficial handwritten statement of transfer of 569 Lenora Street property between Victoria Martino and Joseph Gallippi before the sale was made legal

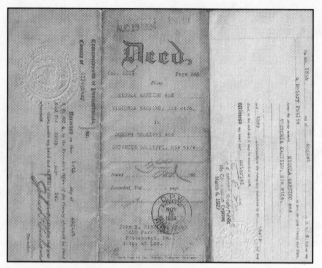

Deed Transfer of 569 Lenora Street property from Nicola & Victoria Martino to Giuseppe & Catarina Gallippi

This Mortgage

Made the 16th day of August in the year of our Lord one thousand nine hundred and Twenty Four (1924).

Between Joseph Gallippi and Catarina Gallippi, his wife, of the City of Pittsburgh, County of Allegheny and State of Pennsylvania, the

mortgagors to the

Liberty--Building and Loan Association, Number Five of Pittsburgh, Allegheny County, Pennsylvania, a corporation of the State of Pennsylvania mortgagee.

Whereas, The said mortgagors by their bond of even date herewith, stand bound unto the mortgagee aforesaid, in the sum of Three Thousand ($3000.00)

Dollars, conditioned for the payment

of Fifteen Hundred ($1500.00) Dollars

with interest, dues and premiums, and such fines as may be imposed, under the by-laws of said mortgagee in the manner and form prescribed in said bond; and all taxes and municipal charges now or hereafter, assessed or charged against the mortgaged premises, penalties and costs, and all premiums and charges for such insurance on the mortgaged buildings as shall be taken out by the mortgagee or assigns, which if paid by the mortgagee or assigns may be added to said real debt; and also, in case of default all fees, costs and expenses of collection including an attorney's commission of Five per cent.

Giuseppe & Catarina's Mortgage for $3,000 at 5% interest was paid off in less than three years

The Gallippi family continued to flourish in the Larimer Avenue Village. The wages Giuseppe began earning at the railroad were a significant improvement from his previous earnings at Highland Park. The grocery store operating from the front porch at 3 Meadow Street eventually fell victim to competition. Giuseppe decided to end that venture when the Labriola family opened their expanded grocery store on Larimer Ave. However, Giuseppe continued operating the olive oil import business, possibly selling some of the oil to the Labriolas. When the family moved to 569 Lenora Street in the heat of August, 1924, Catarina planned her gardens. The long, sloping backyard came complete with peach trees, was perfect for growing vegetables, and raising chickens and pigs. Giuseppe brought home discarded railroad ties[82] and used them to terrace the sloping back yard of their Lenora Street home.

The family ate well as Catarina made fresh pasta, breads, vegetables, soups and sauces using family produced olive oil when needed. Tomatoes, spices, greens and peaches were grown in the backyard and preserved for use all year long. Giuseppe built a pigpen and a chicken coop on the property. The family raised one pig at a time to provide bacon, pork meat and salt-preserved ham. The pig would be shared with extended family and friends who contributed their garbage to feed the pig until it was ready for slaughter. Fat from the pig was rendered and used to make lard for baking. Soap was made from lard mixed with coal ash to harden it. It was used in bar form *(scented with oils from flowers grown on the property)* for bathing; and, in shaved chip form, used for laundry. Chickens were raised for a variety of uses that included soups, meat for main meals and eggs year-round. With the exception of milk and flour, the Gallippi household was a self-sustaining food and recycling factory. Flour was purchased in 50 pound sacks at Labriola's. The dairy farms located on the outskirts of the Larimer Avenue Village provided home delivered milk by the 'The Milk Man'. Milk was not homogenized in those days and the cream rose to the top of the bottle sitting snugly in its narrowed neck. On very cold winter days, the cream would breach the top of the glass bottle pushing up the little white cardboard tab used for a cap.

A 90-year-old piece of Catarina's lard soap preserved by family

Cooking was done on a gas stove and heat was provided by a coal-fired furnace. The same fellow who was 'The Iceman' in the summer became 'The Coal Man' in the winter. In his horse-drawn wagon, he would pick up coal that was shipped in by rail in the winter; and, ice blocks packed in sawdust that were shipped from the great lakes in the summer. There is a family story about Catarina becoming angry at that fellow because he raised the price of coal. She instructed three of her boys to run after the coal wagon and taunt the man, making him mad enough to throw chunks of coal at them. Of course, the kids were then instructed to pick up the chunks of coal and give them to Mama. Many of these memories were shared and became family legend.

One shared legend told of Giuseppe preparing to kill the pig that had grown fat eating garbage. The story goes...on the day the pig was to be killed, Giuseppe aimed his sharply-honed ax at the front of the pig's head with the intent to land it between the eyes to kill it instantly. Giuseppe missed. The wounded pig turned on him chasing him around the pen. Unfortunately for Giuseppe, he couldn't jump out of the pen because eight of his children had gathered around the perimeter and were enjoying the show. Giuseppe frantically waved and shouted for them to get out of the way; but, the kids were too busy laughing at the spectacle. It wasn't until Catarina heard the ruckus and came out to move the children away from the pen that Giuseppe jumped out and was saved.

Giuseppe's Last Days

After working on the railroad for seven years, Giuseppe became ill. His lungs were subjected daily to the fine coal dust in the train engine compartment and it took its toll. Inhaling coal dust for so many years weakened his lungs. Giuseppe's energy began to fade in 1928 and by mid-May of 1929, he fell ill with pneumonia. Catarina tried in vain to nurse him back to health; but, with no success. Doctors at that time were helpless. Penicillin had not yet been discovered and used to treat pneumonia in 1929.

Giuseppe died on June 25, 1929 at 52 years old. He was buried in Mt. Carmel Cemetery at the edge of the Larimer Avenue Village.

Giuseppe did not live to see the American Stock Market crash in September of 1929, three months after he died. Fortunately for the family, and due to his mistrust of American banks, he sent money earned from his side business ventures to the *"Casaforta"* in Filogaso for safekeeping. Money also was kept in their house, layered in the folds of Catarina's clothing treasures stored in her cedar chest. Family recollects money was lost on the last shipment of olives from Italy that rotted on the New York dock in May of 1929, when the price of stocks dropped, causing a minor panic that preceded the major crash. In the panic, there was no one to load the shipment on a train to Pittsburgh as had been customarily done.

Catarina Survives the Loss of her Beloved Husband

Catarina's strength can only be seen as remarkable. Remember, she had no formal education, could not read or write, only spoke Italian and knew no English. She had always been protected by surrounding family. However, she had an important quality and that was not to see herself as a victim. She had natural survival skills and took the initiative to find ways to bring money into the home to feed and to finish raising her children. By approaching the men who owned Larimer Avenue Village construction businesses, Catarina made work arrangements for her sons. The East Liberty Area, of which the Larimer Avenue Village was a part, was considered the mecca of Italian artisans. Stone cutters, marble setters, cabinet makers, brick layers and plasterers all used their skills, and a vast majority worked for Italian-owned businesses. In 1928 there were thirty-eight building contractors, fourteen cement contractors, twenty-two concrete construction contractors, and six marble-cutting businesses. Examples of construction contractors were Massaro, Graziano, Navarro, Zambrano, Ionadi and Dozzi. Marble cutters included Modena, Fornaser, Battista and Rampa. Other skilled workers included barbers, cobblers and tailors.[83]

Catarina had arranged for her oldest son, Anthony James (Tony) to begin an apprenticeship as a plasterer when Giuseppe's health began to fail. Tony had been working as a laborer with no defined skills at the time. He was 21 when Giuseppe died. He became a 'master plasterer', joining a union and worked for a building company. Tony was able to provide income to sustain the family in short order.

Catarina set up an apprentice program for Jimmy, then 19, to work as a marble setter by approaching the owner of the *"Pittsburgh Marble Company"*. The apprenticeship was short, because Jimmy was a quick study. He already had experience working as a carpenter on a number of jobs from the time he left school at 14.

Now two sons were earning money for the family.

1930 U.S. Federal Census shows professions for
Catarina's sons Anthony and Jimmy

Alimina, who by that time went by the nick name "Mimi", and Virginia, who by then was called "Gina", were told they had to quit school immediately no matter what grade they were in. Catarina felt attending school to the 8th grade was enough education for them. Rose, the oldest girl, accompanied by her mother and sisters, went to businesses where Caterina felt they could learn a skill that would give them a better opportunity to earn more money. As a result, 18-year-old Rose, was trained in night school as a switchboard operator for the *"Postal Telegraph Cable Company"*; Mimi, at 16, worked for Sears and Roebuck, the retail giant at that time; and Gina, at 14, learned banking. Soon each was earning a wage to contribute to the family. Benedetto (Benny) was only 12 when Giuseppe died and was encouraged by Catarina to continue his education in a seminary to become a priest. There is no available documentation as to exactly how old Benny was when he entered the seminary; but, we do know he remained there until his mid-20's when he decided the priesthood was not the life for him. Emilio (Emil) and Adelina, (called Adeline and Babe), were still very young and were allowed to remain in school as they had not yet reached the 8th grade. Until more earnings started flowing into the household, the family survived on the money held in the *"Casaforta"* in Filogaso. Catarina did miss out on the small pension provided to the family by the railroad because she had never seen a paper check. When one of these strange looking pieces of paper arrived in the mail she took it to the neighborhood "patron" who assured her he would handle it for her and said whenever she got a paper like this she should just to bring it to him. In short, he stole the money of a widowed woman with children, and most probably a lot of other money as well. By the time Emil and Adeline reached the 8th grade, the family was surviving with everyone's income and the two were allowed to complete high school. In fact, Adeline received a *"Certificate of Perfect Attendance"* from the Commonwealth of Pennsylvania Department of Public Instruction for her perfect attendance in 1932. The others eventually earned their GED High School Diplomas as adults through night school, and Tony went on to earn a two-year degree in Drafting & Architecture from Carnegie Institute of Technology, a college in Oakland, Pittsburgh.

" Saml jr (Emma) jwlr 929 Liberty av h5418 Albemarle
" Walter N clk r344 Semple
Gallino Felix (Felix Beauty Shoppe) r38 Oakland sq
" Lydia hlpr r28 Oakland sq
Gallion Nicholas (Carrick Printing Co) r109 Calhoun av
Gallippi Anthony lab r569 Lenora
" Cath (wid Jos) h569 Lenora
" Domineck (Josephine) confr 126 StClair N h421 Beatty N
" Jas lab r569 Lenora
" Rose opr Postal Teleg-Cable Co r569 Lenora
Gallisath Clementine Mrs r221 Edmond
" Margt slswn Oppenheim Collins & Co r221 Edmond
" Sylvester B clk r221 Edmond
Gallishen Anna emp Stouffer Lunch Inc r523 Saline
" John (Agnes) lab h523 Saline
" John (Mary) lab h523 Saline
" Michl emp Pittsburgh News Ticker Co r523 Saline
Galliso John lab r937 North Lincoln av
" Marie r937 North Lincoln av
" Mary (wd John) h937 North Lincoln av
Gallivan Bessie (wid John) h3431 Bigelow blvd
Gallman Carl musician r352 Prince
" Harriet dom r352 Prince
" Jas driver h352 Prince
" Magnolia r352 Prince
" Rose B dom r352 Prince
Gallo Angelo (Theresa) lab h505 (305) Path way
" Anthony (Rose) lab r167 Mayflower
" Aug clk PO r522 Chester av
" Betty dom 1342 Sheridan
" C Arth clk A G Spalding & Bros r2827 Midland av
" Carmelo (Agnes) lab h5150 Butler

Rose listed as a Postal Telegraph Operator in 1929 Census

Adeline's Perfect Attendance Certificate 1932

Adeline

Jimmy

Catarina & Tony

Benny in Seminary in 1943

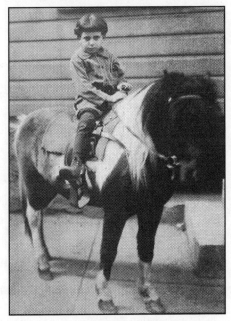

4-year-old Emilio in 1922 poses for picture on "traveling pony" visiting Larimer Village neighborhood

(L-R) Gina, Rose, Catarina, Mimi & Adeline in the early 1940's

Emil at 18 in high school graduation picture

CHAPTER 4

ANTHONY GAETANO'S STORY CONTINUES

Reflections on the year 1906, reveal how the Gallippi's and the Gaetano's lives melded into the Larimer Avenue Village. That was the year Giuseppe Gallippi brought his family to America and the year Antonio Gaetano became a Naturalized American Citizen. In the 11 years Antonio lived in America, financial progress and stability had come to the Gaetano's. Vincenzo, Maria and Antonio, saved enough money to purchase a home at #8 Clay Alley. Each man had contributed a portion of his savings, and coupled with all the money Maria made as a seamstress, $500 was available to use as a down payment. Vincenzo and Maria would live in the first floor, two bedroom apartment of the large house, and Antonio would live in the second floor apartment.

America's economic stability in 1906 made it easy for the Gaetano and the Rizzo families to reach for home ownership. The Federal Reserve was formed to regulate the money supply and *'The Gold Standard Act'* guaranteed gold would be the exclusive backer of US currency, not silver as it was in 1900. Interest rates were controlled instead of moving wildly at the will of the banks.[84] In this low mortgage rate environment, a record of steady employment qualified a man for a $2,000 mortgage loan to purchase a home that cost $2,500. *(Credit reporting agencies were not yet in existence.)*

Antonio Gaetano Becomes a Naturalized Citizen

In 1906 Antonio was ready to become a Naturalized Citizen of his adopted country. His hourly wage was growing and he had the comfort of having his own apartment. Also, *'The Naturalization Act of 1906'* was a bill the United States Congress scheduled for a vote on June 29th of that year. It required immigrants learning English in order to become naturalized citizens and be tested on their English skills. While Antonio felt he had enough English writing and speaking skills to pass such a test, this was too important to take a chance on not passing the test. So, on January 6, 1906, at 26-years-old Antonio Gaetano became a naturalized American citizen.

Antonio Gaetano's Official Naturalization Papers

A History Note-The 1906 Immigration Act

The Bureau of Immigration and Naturalization (INS) was established under *"The Immigration Act of 1906'* within which the first uniform naturalization laws in the country were created. Prior to 1906, an alien could be naturalized in any *'U.S. Court of Record'*.

The Naturalization Act took effect on September 27, 1906. Once enacted, naturalization could only be done in courts authorized to have an Official Seal and a Trained Clerk. The 1906 Act included some quirky elements one of which was that homosexuality was grounds for exclusion from both immigration and naturalization. Given the 2014 United States Supreme Court ruling on equality for same sex couples under the law, and the public discussion, both, pro and con on the acceptance of homosexuality, this piece of history discovered during research seemed interesting enough to note.[85] This portion of the 1906 Act would not be modified until *'The Immigration Act of 1990'* when homosexuality was removed as grounds for exclusion. In addition, the modification included exceptions to the English testing process required for naturalization set forth by *'The Naturalization Act of 1906'*.[86]

Antonio Gaetano Takes a Wife

Comfortably secured as a citizen of the United States, in 1907 Antonio was ready to cross the Atlantic Ocean to seek a wife. He was not concerned about temporarily leaving his job with the gas company as work was abundant in Pittsburgh and his relationship with his boss was solid.

Through correspondence with an uncle in Nicastro, a marriage was arranged. **Rosa Gaetano,** Antonio's first cousin who was the daughter of his Uncle Vincenzo, would be his wife.

CHAPTER 5

VOYAGER ROSA GAETANO GAETANO
(June 9, 1889 – June 1, 1970)

The Reluctant Rosa

Rosa Gaetano was the oldest daughter of **Concette Amendola** *(born September 21, 1853)* and **Vincenzo Gaetano** *(birthdate unknown)*. Rosa's father arranged her marriage to his brother Bruno's son **Antonio Gaetano**. She was 18-years-old at the time and was not interested in marrying her first cousin as she had fallen in love with a handsome man in her village of Nicastro, Italy. When Antonio arrived in Nicastro from America to collect his chosen bride, he was not met with warmth from Rosa. Antonio waited for a year until she agreed to marry him after much cajoling by her family. The marriage to Antonio became an issue of honor for the family as *'arrangements had been made'*. Antonio felt the fight for her affection was worth it. From the first moments he saw the handsome Rosa walking from the fish fountain carrying the "catch of the day" he was smitten. She was a striking beauty with a narrow waist, jet black hair, flawless skin, and dark eyes.

Rosa Gaetano at 19 years old in 1908

Family verbal history tells of Rosa being pampered by her mother and father as she was their first born child. History on Rosa's father Vincenzo is vague with the exception of his relationship to his nephew Antonio. However, information on her mother's family, the Amendola's, was bountiful. Her mother Concette was a respected woman in her village. She was the 'healer' and 'midwife' who had knowledge of medicines using a collection of herbs and treatments on villagers who were sick. Rosa's Grandmother was **Teresa Mannarino Amendola** *(born May 24, 1831)* and her grandfather was **Domenico Maria Amendola** *(born May 2, 1822)*. Information on Rosa's brother **Vincenzo Gaetano** *(January 12, 1896-September 13, 1980)* was verified when, in 1985, Rosa's daughter Catherine and her husband Tony Gallippi traveled to Nicastro from Pittsburgh to find family members some 60 years after the family emigrated to America. Vincenzo's funeral card containing information about him was given to them by family members.

On that same trip, Rosa's younger sister **Teodora Gaetano** *(birthdate unknown)* was discovered living in Milano, Italy with her children. She is deceased at this writing and the exact date of her death is not known.

Great Aunt Teodoro pictured with family in Milano in 1985

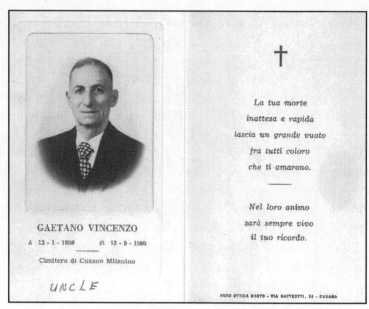

Great Uncle Vincenzo Gaetano Rosa Gaetano's Brother

Great Uncle Vincenzo's son and Rosa's nephew Antonio in 1942.
(September 9, 1923 - June 25, 1986)

Great Aunt Teodoro Picture taken in 1969

The Amendola Family

The Amendola family had roots in Paola, Cosenza, Calabria, Italy when Rosa's great, great, great grandparents **Saverio Amendola** and his wife **Cayetana Bresco** emigrated from Argentina to Italy in 1645. This is documented; however, there is a gap in information between that emigration and the date Rosa's great, great grandfather **Francesco Saverio Amendola** *(1758-1828)* was born. The pieces fit when dates on the documentation of the woman Francesco married, **Anna Garritano** *(1760-April 11, 1830),* proved her parents were **Filippo Garritano** *(1793-1841)* and **Teresa Donato** showing a logical 48-year-gap between generations.

Francesco Saverio Amendola had a son named **Antonio Maria Amendola** *(1775-December 15, 1849)* who married **Maria Serafina Mannarino** (1808-1843). They were Rosa's great grandparents. Antonio Maria was 25-years-old and Maria Serafina was 13-years old when they married on January 21, 1821 in Paola. Records show Maria Serafina Mannarino's parents were **Pasquale Mannarino and Caterina Leone.**

Five children were born to Antonio Maria and Maria Serafina. Their first child, named Concette, lived to only 10 years *(1842-1852);* **Domenico Maria Amendola** (Rosa's grandfather); and Rosa's three uncles - **Salvatore Amendola** *(born December 13, 1863);* **Giuseppe Amendola** *(born September 20, 1870);* and **Giovanni Amendola** *(born January 16, 1875).*
(See Amendola family tree on page 101)
NOTE: Dates were listed as verified in documents. In some cases there was only a birth date and no death date, in some cases only the year was listed)

Why Rosa's great grandparents Domenico Maria and Maria Serafina Amendola moved south from Paola, Cosenza to Nicastro around 1860 is not clear either in the records or by family recollection. The two areas are in the Region of Calabria. One could speculate a reason was the climate. Completely surrounded by mountains, Cosenza's

Rose Gaetano's Family Tree – The Amendola Family

Great, Great, Great, Great, Great Grandparents
Saverio Amendola & Cayetana Bresco
(Emigrated from Argentina to Paola, Cosenza, Calabria, Italy in 1645)

(Information missing)

Great, Great, Great, Great Grandparents
Francesco Saverio Amendola & Anna Garritano >
(1758-September 8, 1858)   (1760-April 1830 @ 70 years old)
(Both born in Longobardi, Cosenza, Calabria - Both died in Paola, Cosenza, Calabria.)

Filippo Garritano & Teresa Donato
(1793 – 1841) (parents of Anna Garritano)

<Anna Garritano

Dominica M. (married) **Pasqual Amendola**
Married July 16, 1812

Angela Maria Amendola (married) **Antonio Maria Bruno**
(1800-1822)   (Vincenzo Bruno & Anna Maria Filippo's son)

Giuseppe Amendola (married) **Angela Marie D'Andrea**
(1789-1833)   July 26, 1812   (1797-1862)

Isadora Amendola (born November 18, 1837)

Great, Great, Great Grandparents

Antonio Maria Amendola (married) **Maria Serafina Mannarino** (daughter of **Pasquale Mannarino & Catherine Leone**)
(1796 – December 15, 1849)   (1808-1843)
Married January 21, 1821 in Paola, Cosenza, Calabria – Antonio was 25 and Maria Serafina was 13 years old

Salvatore Amendola (born December 13, 1863)
Giuseppe Amendola (born September 20, 1870)
Giovanni Amendola (born January 16, 1875)

Great, Great Grandparents
Domenico M. Amendola (married) **Teresa Mannarino**
(born May 2, 1822)   (born May 24, 1831)

Great Grandparents
Concetta Amendola (married) **Vincenzo Gaetano**
(Born Sept. 21, 1853)   (birthdate unknown)

Grandparents- Parents of Catherine Maria Gaetano
Rosa Gaetano (married) **Antonio Gaetano**
(June 9, 1889-June 1, 1970) (July 3, 1880-July 4, 1930)
Mother

Vincenzo
(January 12, 1896-September 13, 1980)

Theodora Vescio
(dates unknown)

Concetta
(1812-1852)

Bruno
(1909-1924)

Vincenzo
(1911-1911)

Catherine Marie
(1914-)
Janet   Doris

Antonio
(1921-1979)
Karen   Anthony

Maria
(1922-1972)
Joan   Carol   Maria

Michael
(1924-1982)

Bruno the younger
(1926-19--)
Louis   John   Rosemarie

not influenced by the Mediterranean Sea, having cold winters and hot summers. Whereas, Nicastro's climate reaped the influence of the Mediterranean and was more favorable. Another reason could have been the political climate in Italy at that location. Occupied by the Spanish army from the 1500's, the Austrians in 1707, having fought against French domination from 1806 to 1815 and ultimately the local riots of 1821 and 1837 heralded by Risorgimento, Cosenza had seen its measure of strife. It seems logical finding a more peaceful place to live would have occurred to its residents. It was in Nicastro, by arranged marriage, Rosa's mother Concette Amendola married Rosa's father Vincenzo Gaetano.

The Wedding of Antonio and Rosa

In 1908, 19-year-old, 4' 11" tall Rosa Gaetano married the 5'11" tall Antonio Gaetano in St. Antonio Di Padova Church in Nicastro, all the while yearning for the man she loved. Given the status of her family, Rosa's wedding was a village social affair. For her wedding she was dressed in the traditional native style of the village. The dress was made of a fine quality black silk material accompanied by the traditional white cape with its delicate fringe draped softly on her shoulders. Around her neck was a black velvet band. The sleeves of the dress were fitted to her slender arms and of a three-quarter length. The same style of lace fringe on the cape was sewn to and draped below the end of the sleeve. Her veil, worn during the church ceremony, was attached at the crown of her upswept jet-black hair, covering her face and leaving her dark eyes and delicate lips barely visible. She carried a

Antonio and Rosa's official wedding photo

bouquet of freshly picked wild flowers arranged by her cousin Angela Maria Amendola for the occasion. It is said Rosa smiled once or twice throughout the festivities as relatives wished the newly-married couple well and handed them gifts of hand-made doilies, homemade treats and bottles of vino.

Left is an example of a traditional Nicastro Village wedding dress. Right is traditional dress worn by Village women

St. Anthony Di Padova Roman Catholic Church in Nicastro where Antonio and Rosa were married

The Altar at St. Anthony Di Padova Roman
Catholic Church in Nicastro, Italy

By the time their first son, **Bruno** was born in 1909, Antonio was anxious to return to America; but, Rosa was not.

In 1911, a second son, **Vincenzo** was born and died at one month old during a convulsion. In her emotional state, Rosa again refused to go to America as Antonio's concerns about little work and less money mounted. He was weary of living in Italy because he could see nothing had changed for the wage earner. Antonio was discouraged and knowing the loneliness that awaited him, left for Naples where he boarded a steamship back to America and the Larimer Avenue Village. His only positive thought was he knew, as a naturalized American citizen, he didn't have to go through the entire process at Ellis Island again.

Rosa, 10-month old Bruno, and Antonio in Nicastro in 1910. Rosa was pregnant with their second son Vincenzo

Home in America

When Antonio's steamship docked in New York, he showed his citizenship papers and made his way to Pittsburgh without interruption. Uncle Domenico consoled Antonio telling him many wives were hesitant to come to America because it was difficult for them to leave the only family they had known. He felt the best medicine for Antonio was to return to work. Fortunately, there was a demand for laborers at the gas company as gas remained the primary source of energy for cooking and heating water. It was a more efficient way of supplying fuel. The demand continued because George Westinghouse had purchased regional gas fields providing the means for extending pipelines to municipalities in the greater Pittsburgh area.

Antonio would not give up on having his family come to America. In 1913 he returned to Nicastro to try to convince Rosa to come to America. On February 27, 1914 his first daughter, **Catherine Marie,** was born. Rosa was steadfast in her decision not to go to America. Antonio stayed in Italy until his young daughter was a year old and returned to America in 1915 without his family for the same financial concerns. Again, he was able to resume work with the gas company; however, his employment with them would end when he returned to Italy in 1919. By that time Catherine Marie was 5-years-old and Bruno was 10-years-old.

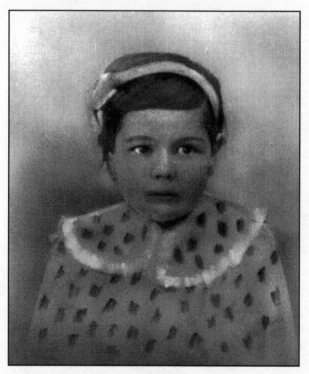

Catherine Marie at 3 years

Catherine Marie at 3-years-old with her big brother Bruno at 10-years-old

In November of 1920, their fourth child, **Antonio** was born, and in December of 1922 their fifth child, **Maria** was born. Again, the pampered Rosa flatly refused to return to America with Antonio. She was comfortable living in her apartment in Nicastro adjacent to her mother and father's apartment.

As stated earlier, little official information on Rosa's father Vincenzo was available at this writing however, the childhood memories of his granddaughter Catherine Marie provide an image of the man. She remembered her grandfather as being "a very strong man with a big mustache". She said Vincenzo was a farmer who took his donkey to the field everyday to tend his crops. Two deep wicker baskets straddled the donkey's back, carrying items to the plot and the fruits of his labor back home for the family. She remembers eating his fresh vegetables, fruit, olives and figs. Each day, when her mother would let her, she would wait for him to return home and run to the end of the stone path to their home so he could lift her up and put her in one of the baskets to ride the donkey for the rest of his walk home. Catherine Marie also remembered the closeness she had with her grandparents as their apartments were connected by a door she could easily open in the early morning to climb into their warm bed snuggling between them.

Pictured above are the doors to Rosa's and her parent's apartments that opened to a common balcony

There was no schooling for young children in Nicastro. Neither Catherine Marie nor her older brother Bruno were taught to read or write. At age 8, Bruno began going to the farm plot with his grandfather to learn how to plant and tend to fig trees as it was assumed he, too, would be a farmer. Life in Nicastro centered on the family and the church. Religious customs were interwoven into the family activities. Catherine Marie would accompany her grandmother to the Shrine in Nicastro to pray daily. Catherine Marie was chosen many times to attend baptisms of babies born in their village as it was customary to have a young 'virgin' present to symbolize the purity of the child. By all accounts, the family was happy and Rosa had no intention or incentive to move out of her comfort zone since Antonio was providing money for the family to live in Italy.

Pictured above are the doors to Rosa's and her parents apartments that opened to a common balcony

U.S. *"Emergency Quota Act"* **Affects Rosa's Life**

Rosa's comfort and strong convictions were to come to an end when the U.S. government announced it planned to close Ellis Island and end immigration to America with the 1921 *"Emergency Quota Act"*. *"The National Origins Act"* would close Ellis Island to immigration in 1924. Not only was the tide of history against Rosa's strong will; her mother and grandmother's opinions also went against Rosa's desires. Even though it is said they were heartbroken to lose her, they insisted she go to America to live with her husband because she had 4 children and she 'belonged' to him.

Rosa and the children would have to make the voyage alone. Antonio used his savings traveling back and forth to try to get her to agree to emigrate. In America, Antonio made arrangements for their passage that included securing a U.S. Passport for her and the children. Also, his source of income by then had shifted as the demand for gas company laborers waned. There is no record of where he worked after he left the gas company and until his employment at the Highland Park Zoo feeding the big cats, a job he secured in 1922. It is presumed he held a number of jobs as a laborer for a series of different projects. Pittsburgh was loaded with opportunities for laborers, skilled and unskilled, to build roadways, railroads, and buildings. There were jobs working in the mills, mines and factories. In fact, companies were still sending job recruiters through rural areas in Italy, hiring peasants to work in the United States. Many family members and residents of the same village rushed to emigrate and encouraged family members and friends to follow.[87]

Rosa's Passport Application

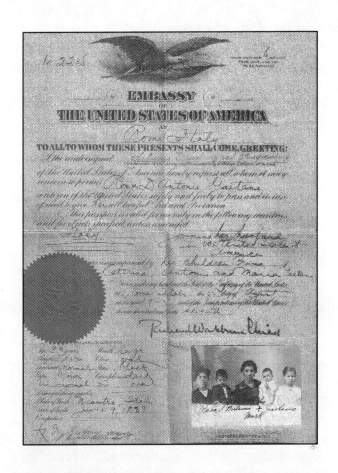

Enlarged Passport Picture

Preparations for Rosa's Voyage

Getting the then 33-year-old Rosa and the children ready to make the voyage to America was a major production involving her mother, grandparents, aunts and uncles. She took the children to St. Antonio Church for their 'final blessings' making sure Bruno and Catherine received the sacrament of Confirmation. She reached out for personal strength from everyone around her. She was finicky about what she brought with her and didn't understand the restrictions on the amount of luggage she was allowed to bring or could have carried for her. After all, her arms would be filled with children, not luggage. She insisted Antonio make arrangements to have her luggage carried for her as she boarded the steamship *"SS Colombo"* from the port at Naples, Italy in September of 1922. In her luggage were linens, homemade throw rugs and clothing she had made for the children and herself.

By then, **Bruno** was 13-years-old, **Catherine** was 8-years-old, **Antonio** was 20-months-old and **Maria** was 9-months-old. Catherine clearly remembered this portion of her life and her 12-day voyage. She talked about it often to her children after she married Tony Gallippi in 1936. She remembered her mother's fear and deep sadness as she was leaving the security of her parents and village. She talked of her grandmother's tears streaming down her cheeks as the family began boarding the ship and of her grandmother putting her hands on Catherine's shoulders, their eyes connecting for a last look, saying she would never see Catherine again. Catherine remembered, in her child-like way saying, *"Nonna, they say sometimes the weather doesn't agree with people in America and they come back. If that happens, I will be back."* Those were the last words Catherine ever spoke to her grandmother, and she remembered standing on the deck of the ship waving as her grandmother got smaller in the distance as the ship set sail.

The Voyage

Soon the family settled into their places in the steerage section of the ship with some 1,000 others who were making that same voyage. There was nothing dignified about traveling in steerage. Rosa, on her own for the first time in her life, grouped her children around her in what she felt would be a safe and comfortable space.

"The Ellis Island Oral History Project"

Paul Eugene Sigrist, Oral Historian, Ellis Island

At the urging of her daughter Janet, Catherine, at 76-years-old, participated in a project designed to re-create the history of emigration at the Island through the United States Department of the Interior National Park Service, Statue of Liberty National Monument Liberty Island, New York, New York 10004. She was interviewed in 1990 by Paul Eugene Sigrist, Jr., Oral Historian for the U.S. Department of the Interior National Park Service. Catherine's verbal account of her voyage is a permanent part of that history. It can be accessed through the Ellis Island website or in person at Ellis Island.

Highlights of the verbal history include Catherine's account of a 'pretty lady', traveling first class, dressed in silk finery and cloaked in a fur wrap. She 'took a liking' to Catherine who was spending an hour on the fresh air deck with her mother, brothers and sister. The woman sent a message with a crew member to ask Rosa if it would be okay for Catherine to join her in a stroll around the deck and dinner, suggesting it would provide some relief for Rosa who had young children to care for. Rosa agreed. Catherine put on her best dress, was escorted up several, narrow metal stairwells to the upper deck.

Rosa was accustomed to people being attracted to Catherine. Many times in Italy, in preparation for a traditional baptism ceremony, Catherine was sought out to attend, holding a white lily as a symbol of the purity of a virginal child.

Catherine was greeted by the woman (whose name she could not remember) for a stroll around the deck and to Catherine's surprise, the stroll ended with dinner at the Captain's table. Catherine remembers the large round table dressed in white linens and fancy dishes filled with foods she had never seen.

She remembers being introduced to the Captain wearing his white uniform with gold trim, and the other adults at the table who were delighted to have a child join them. She made it through the dinner with her impeccable manners that were very much a part of Rosa's grooming. Catherine, always the caretaker, politely asked the lady if it would be okay to bring some of the leftover food to her mother and family below. The Captain overheard the request and, after dinner, ordered a shipmate to collect an assortment of foods for the family. Catherine and the basket of food were escorted back to her mother in steerage. Catherine remembers handing the foods to her mother and the pleasure on her mother's face.

Catherine also remembered all the steps the family went through during processing at Ellis, and being greeted by her father in the **'Kissing Room'**. A very excited Antonio had a cab waiting to transport the family from the dock to the train for the long ride to the Larimer Avenue Village.

Rosa and Children Arrive in Pittsburgh

The fragile-natured Rosa was mortified when she entered smog-filled Pittsburgh and wanted to return to Italy immediately. Of course, that was not possible. That first impression was talked about frequently and remained with Rosa into her later years along with the fact that she didn't have her 'beautiful' furniture anymore.

The family occupied the top two floors of the house on Clay Alley. Uncle Domenico and Aunt Maria, who were living below, did everything possible to make Rosa comfortable and help her adjust to her new life. Antonio, feeling the stress of Rosa's disappointment, bought her a large-stoned garnet ring mounted on a 10K gold band to make her feel better. The ring became a symbol of Rosa's emigration to America.

Larimer Avenue Village-The 'Little Italy' of Pittsburgh

Rosa arrived to a bustling Italian neighborhood documented as Pittsburgh's largest *'Little Italy'* housing over 2,755 foreign-born residents. When the children of these residents were counted the community numbered 6,061 people.[88] As emigration waned after 1924, the community of Italians in the Larimer Avenue Village unified, feeling they would be the last ones to come to the village.

Although her new home did not resemble her sunny little village of Nicastro, Rosa did her best to adjust. Aunt Maria took Rosa to Larimer Avenue where she could see Labriola's Grocery Store, Giganti's Butcher Shop and the many other shops where Italian foods like olives, olive oil, cheeses, fresh sausage and Bacala were sold. And, of course, there was Moio's, the bakery supreme for pastry. Other bakeries like Stagno's sold fresh bread daily. Rosa started to feel at home. Many of her initial fears had passed when she discovered everyone spoke Italian and many of her neighbors had come from the Calabria Region of Italy. There was much conversation to be enjoyed with the other women in the village who had made the transition to America. During this time, Antonio worked 6-days-a week at the Highland Park Zoo, earning enough money for the family to live comfortably.

Antonio, in his progressive way, insisted both Bruno and Catherine attend Our Lady Help of Christian Church School against Rosa's wishes. He wanted them to learn to read and write in English so they could benefit from all that America had to offer. Catherine remembers being taught by the Nuns at the school, and because she was a good student, was used as an example for other children who were not performing well. She was 8-years-old in 1st grade, learned English quickly, and soon skipped a grade or two as her language and reading skills improved. Catherine spoke of her love of school, her love of reading, and the doors of knowledge that were opened to her. She often reflected in her later years at how different it was from Italy where girls only learned to sew and cook; and, how different her life would have been if she remained in her village of Nicastro, Italy.

13-year-old Bruno (4th from the right in the center row) posed with his classmates at Our Lady Help of Christian Church School in 1922

1924...A year of Happiness and Tragedy

Happiness came to Rosa and Antonio in June of 1924 when their 6th child, **Angelo (Michael) Gaetano** was born. For Antonio this was cause for celebration because Michael was the first of his children to be born in America. But, this happiness was not to be sustained. Just 6 months after Michael was born, tragedy struck. Antonio and Rosa's oldest son, Bruno, at age 15 while riding his bike on the Highland Avenue Bridge, was struck by a vehicle and killed. He suffered internal injuries when the handlebar of the bicycle pierced his abdomen. He died 24 hours later in Pittsburgh Hospital. It was a bitterly cold November day in 1924.

Rosa collapsed. She had lost her son and verbally cursed America for the tragedy. She slipped into a deep depression and spent nearly 6 months in bed while 10-year-old Catherine kept the household together, caring for her baby brother Michael and her other siblings. Aunt Maria prepared dinner for the family daily. Catherine scarcely went to school that year, and weathered a tug of war between her mother, who wanted her to quit altogether to care for the family, and her father, who made arrangements for her to continue her education by having a Nun come to the house to tutor Catherine in the evenings. Antonio made it his business to be around during the tutoring to assure himself Rosa would not interfere and to reassure Catherine it was okay to study while her mother was ill.

By all accounts it was a dark time for the family; but, Rosa finally regained her strength and began to function as Antonio's wife and the mother of the household again. She and Antonio had their 7th child in 1925 and named him **Bruno** after the son who died. The family had new life for the first time in a long time. Below is the 1925 picture of the entire family in which Rosa was pregnant with Bruno the younger.

Pictured are Antonio, holding 9-month-old Michael; 4-year-old Antonio; Rosa, pregnant with Bruno the younger; 2-year-old Maria; and 11-year-old Catherine

Antonio and the Big Cat

Catherine remembers going to Highland Park with her family and seeing her father work with the big cats at the zoo. She recalled his feeding them and the great roars coming from the lions that scared and excited her at the same time. Most of the time Antonio had no problem with the big cats; but, one day while feeding a particularly hungry lion, he had his left hand in the feeding slot, and was moving the food tray to sit on his flat right hand to slide the tray further into the slot when the lion went for the food. The tip of Antonio's thumb became a tasty morsel for the lion that day.

Good Years for the Gaetano Family

With baby Bruno in arms, the family enjoyed attending church and participating in Larimer Avenue Village events. There were saints' day feasts in which a statue of St. Rocco or St. Anthony was paraded through the streets while residents pinned money to the clothing on the statue. Leading the parade were rows of young children dressed in their first communion clothing carrying long stemmed gladiolas. This custom, brought to the village from the old country, ended with a bandstand event in the 'Club Yard', the ball field at the end of Indiana Way.

There was plenty of old world food, and families gathered for the event. Antonio was earning enough money for the family to move from the small apartment on Clay Street to the house at #5 Meadow Street, next door to the Gallippi family. It was there 11-year-old Catherine first saw 19-year-old Anthony James (Tony), the man who would eventually become her husband. In 1925, Tony was nearly 20 years old. To him she was just the little kid who lived next door.

11-year-old Catherine Gaetano *19-year-old Tony Gallippi*

119

Tragedy Strikes Again

Just when things seemed to be going so well, tragedy struck again in 1929. Antonio had a stroke while working at the zoo. He was found lying motionless on the Highland Park grounds and was taken to the hospital. Rosa was summoned and the news was not good. Antonio was paralyzed on one side of his body; but, that wasn't all. Unknown to Antonio, Rosa or his caretakers, was the fact that Antonio's genetic structure contained an inherited defective gene whose destructive capability was compounded by the stroke. The doctors were puzzled by the characteristics of his declining mental health. *(see "More on the Defective Gene" on page 122)*

Antonio and Rosa Became Destitute

When Antonio became sick, he could not work. There were no longer wages to support the family and there was no health insurance to cover medical expenses. He became a welfare supported patient and was transferred to Mayview Hospital in Pittsburgh for care. At that time nursing homes and mental hospitals were contained in the same building and Mayview was just such a nursing home. It was difficult for Rosa to visit, and strange for her to see mentally ill patients on the same floor with Antonio. There was a social stigma and ignorance regarding mental illness as the condition was thought to be associated with possession by the devil and other superstitions. Rosa's ignorance of the world beyond her doors terrified her with each visit. Catherine, on the other hand, was not terrified. She had been the family's caretaker once before. Where her mother could not even shave her father's face, Catherine would. Where her mother would shy away from other patients at Mayview, Catherine would approach and touch their hands. Deterioration caused by the defective gene eventually caused her father, Antonio Gaetano's death on America's Independence Day, July 4, 1930 just before he reached 50 years old.

One can't help but wonder what Antonio thought as he lay in Mayview Hospital in the last months of his life knowing he was leaving his precious Rosa and children in poverty. Did he reflect on those days back in 1895 when he stood on the deck of the steamship *"SS Patria"* full of hope as he watched giant waves on the Atlantic? It is a good presumption he could not have known he was carrying the genetic trigger that would cause his early death.

Rosa Goes Into Mourning

Again Rosa took to her bed for months leaving her 16-year-old daughter Catherine to care for the home and children. Catherine was the sole caretaker for the family even seeing to it the young children hung their stockings and got Christmas presents from Santa. The family was supported by what was then called *'Mother's Assistance'*, the welfare program of the time. Catherine was counseled by a welfare department's social worker to leave school because she was 16, and take a job as a tailor's apprentice at Frank and Seder's Department Store in East Liberty. It became her job to earn money to support the family. Rosa would occasionally take in some sewing to help but Catherine was the main breadwinner and she quietly resented having to leave the school she grew to love.

The immigrant experience for Rosa and Catarina

Capsulated in Rosa and Catarina's story is a spectrum of the new immigrant experience for women who came to America at the behest of their husbands. Either women of that time welcomed being in America, like Catarina; or, they didn't, like Rosa. Where Catarina never saw herself as a victim and embraced her life in the new country; Rosa did not embrace her life in the new country and always saw herself as a victim.

Rosa never got over the wounds of being torn away from the comfortable life in her home country, from never seeing her mother or father again; and from being forced into a marriage with a man she didn't know and didn't want. There was resentment in Rosa because decisions for her life were made by others without concern for her feelings. That resentment was compounded by the loss of her son and husband shortly after arriving in America. In addition, Rosa was not the type to embrace adventure, perhaps because she had no knowledge of a world outside of her own. First, Rosa's mother and father were her anchors. Then, Rosa's husband Antonio was her anchor. When he got sick and died, she did not know how to help herself or her family. Her third anchor became her daughter Catherine, and her fourth and final anchor became her son Michael. She is in many ways a tragic figure.

Catarina, on the other hand, came from a family of adventurers. Her family was willing to investigate life in more countries than

America, and brought back stories of life in Argentina, Brazil, and Canada. She also married a man she had chosen and loved; and, felt privileged to have a partnership respected by both of them. When her husband Giuseppe died, she was able to adjust to life in America without his guidance. What both women had in common was their need to depend on their children to bring money into the home because of their illiteracy and lack of education. Neither one was financially able to support their family by getting a job of their own. However, it is sad to think that Rosa could not understand how unfair it was for her young daughter Catherine to carry the burden of being the strength of the family...shepherding her mother, brothers and sister along to a place of comfort.

I remember my father once explaining to me that my mother never really had a childhood. He said it as we were watching my mother laugh out loud while enjoying a hayride with my children, her three young grandchildren, **Rosanne, Carolyn** and **Nancy.**

My sister Janet and I, in our young years, didn't fully understand the circumstances of our mother's childhood or the impact Grandma Rosa's weaknesses had on her. It was obvious to us that our mother's attitudes were a little different than our aunts on the Gallippi side of the family. There was both an underlying sadness in our mom and the determination of a strong-willed survivor. Her constant worrying crowded out her happiness some times. Without a doubt there was cause to worry about her family while she helplessly watched them slide into sickess and death. And, there was worry about our finances as our father was a progressive-minded man, who much like his father, would take risks to move us forward. Some of those risks worked and some didn't. Money was not always consistent as his work was primarily in plastering and construction, and sometimes there were gaps in paychecks.

Our mother taught us to be strong like her, and to always find a way to take care of ourselves. She is our hero and truly a woman to be respected and admired. As we care for her in her 101st year, it is with a gentle and understanding hands.

More on the Defective Gene

It was not until the 1960's, that information about the inherited defective gene was revealed. It became known when Antonio's son

Tony, then in his 40's, became ill. His physical decline began with injuries sustained in an explosion of a tool shed filled with dynamite while fighting a fire as a volunteer fireman in his community. The firemen on either side of him perished instantly in the explosion. Tony, as a highly decorated veteran of WWII who had experienced front-line battle action in the invasion at Anzio Beach, was behaving as if he was suffering from being 'shell-shocked'. As his mental health declined, he was transported to a Veterans Hospital in Pittsburgh for extensive care and treatment. After 2 years of care, he died.

The question for his doctors was why would such a young man be presenting the characteristics of senile dementia? The uniqueness of his illness caught the attention of a U.S. government research team in Bethesda, Maryland who traced the family tree back to Italy. The team discovered 125 members of the Gaetano family over several previous generations had inherited a defective gene. They all died from what was called 'pre-senile dementia'. It was learned that Tony's paternal grandmother was the carrier of the gene. She died after being cared for in an Italian nursing facility.

Research revealed that Antonio's younger sister Maria's death, several years before his and in her 40's, also was caused by the defective gene. And, years later, when Antonio's younger brother Michael presented the same symptoms, tests showed he, too, had inherited the defective gene. After Michael was admitted to the same Veterans Hospital where his brother Anthony had died, the Bethesda Research Team was alerted and the research continued. Two years after the onset of the sickness at the age of 46 Michael died in 1972.

The team started contacting living relatives of the deceased family members. Maria's daughter Joan was contacted. She submitted herself to testing at the Bethesda facility. It was determined she had inherited the gene and had a 50-50 chance of become ill. At this writing she is in her upper 60's, happily enjoying life with her long time husband Marty, their children and grandchildren. Upon testing Catherine and Bruno the younger, it was determined neither one of them had inherited the defective gene, and their children and grandchildren did not have to be concerned with its effects. The good news is no other members of this aging family, or their children, have shown any signs of damage from the defective gene.

CHAPTER 6

LIFE IN PITTSBURGH & THE LARIMER AVENUE VILLAGE IN THE 1930's, 1940's & 1950's

After the stock market crash in 1929, America was in a deep depression and everyone was affected by it well into the 1930's. There was no consistent work, no consistent income, and no food for many families. However, the Italian Larimer Avenue community had something positive going for it in the face of this national chaos. They had the homegrown foods from their gardens, and chickens and pigs raised on their land to eat. They shared their food with one another. Sadly, they no longer had the advantage of enjoying their savory, home-made wines because prohibition prompted many Italians to destroy their stocks fearing repercussion from the government.

Some of the stories of legend about Catarina Gallippi's generosity came from this period. She had 8 children to feed and would begin preparing the day's meals at dawn. Every day, homemade pasta was made and dried on flour-dusted, brown paper bags poised on every flat surface in the kitchen. Bread dough was rising in two large, cream-colored crockery bowls topped with tea towels. Sometimes Catarina's sweater topped the tea towels to maintain the necessary warmth for the bread dough to rise. A decision was made about the main meal for the day and either a chicken was killed or preserved pork was made into 'porkettas' *(sliced pork pounded into boneless pieces dipped in egg then breadcrumbs and fried in olive oil)*. Vegetables were picked from the gardens and peaches from trees in summer. In the winter, home-canned items were used. And when enough of the other ingredients were available, Catarina would dig into her supply of lard to make a dessert. Toward sunset, hungry and homeless men would gather outside the door at 569 Lenora Street knowing Mrs. Gallippi would have something for each of them to eat. After the family finished their dinner, the younger children were instructed to bring a leftover item to the door to be given to the hungry men gathered there. Sometimes it was only a piece of bread and sometimes it was a small dish of pasta, or greens or soup that was eaten on the sidewalk just outside the door. They all knew the rules.

Mrs. Gallippi required all bowls, forks and spoons to be left on the stoop when they were finished...and they were.

Subsequent generations would joke about having inherited the 'Generosity Gene' from Nonni. Tony and Jimmy were known for not hesitating to stick their hand in their pocket to give a buck to a guy in need or pay someone's streetcar fare. This legacy was adopted by Catarina's grandchildren. We all felt we had been born to the manor of generosity and small acts of kindness. We grew up knowing it was not only what we were morally bound to do but was tradition.

Even though there was a strain on families of the time, there was a measure of ebullience in this family. A burst of renewed life was experienced by the Gallippi and Gaetano children in the 1930's. By all accounts they were a jovial and fun loving group as their Americanization continued. With widowed, stay-at-home mothers and no fatherly direction, they made their way. The Gallippi children in 1930 were the following ages: Tony was 22 and Jimmy was 21; Rose, Mimi and Virginia ranged in age from 19 to 15; and Benny, Emil and Adeline were 14, 12, & 10 years old. Catherine Gaetano was 16 and her younger siblings were 10, 9, 7 and 5. Catherine and the Gallippi girls 'hung out' together when they were not working. In the early 1930's they would attend dances and social functions at the Kingsley House which by then had moved to a large building on Larimer Avenue. There were mutually-beneficial lodges like *"The Sons and Daughters of Italy Lodge"* touting the *'pride of being an Italian'* philosophy while providing adaptation information and gathering events for their members. There were church functions, the annual St. Anthony's and St. Rocco's Saints' Day Festivals, picnics at Highland Park and trips to the zoo to see the latest attractions. To enhance their Americanization, the girls modernized their appearance.

Young Catherine began calling herself 'Kay' and 'bobbed' her hair opting for the modern, short-waved look. She removed her pierced earrings and wore more fashionable earrings thinking pierced ears marked her as a foreigner. When she could, she would purchase a modern outfit that she would use to design and create more modern clothing for herself. Catherine grew through the dichotomy of being an Italian at home, and an American outside the door of her home. She faced an amazing number of challenges.

Thoroughly Modern 'Kay' with bobbed hair at 20-years-old

Pictured above is an 18-year-old Kay posing in front of the Gaetano family home at 5 Maxwell Way

The Effect of High Culture

An important part of this family's Americanization came from exposure to the 'high culture' of Oakland, PA, located just beyond East Liberty. Oakland was Pittsburgh's predominant cultural and educational center. It had three universities, multiple museums, a huge library, a music hall, a botanical conservatory, and Forbes Field where the Pittsburgh Pirates Baseball Team played from 1909 to 1970.[89] This exposure provided a huge and valuable learning advantage for the maturing families. If they could not have a formal education due to their economic situation, they could dip into a wealth of knowledge in a casual way. There were caverns of information that included visiting current and past history through books and museum exhibits; classical music and opera performed at the Syria Mosque in Oakland; and the beauty of exotic plants at Phipps Conservatory.

Hollywood in East Liberty

The times also were marked by the beginning of the *"Golden Age of Hollywood"* [90] and East Liberty was set up for showing entertaining films in the 8 movie theaters located a streetcar ride away. There was *"Alice in Wonderland"; "Cleopatra"; "The Prisoner of Zenda";* Erroll Flynn as *"Captain Blood";* the antics of the Marx Brothers; Shirley Temple; Clark Gable; Greta Garbo; and William Powell and Myrna Loy in the *"Thin Man"*. There were musicals with gorgeous gowns worn by Betty Grable and fancy dancing by Fred Astaire. Movies were a place to dream romantic dreams.

The Marriages

For the two families romantic dreams became romantic realities in the 1930's. Jimmy married the love of his life **Anna Bertha (Smiley) Seydor** *(born 1914)* when they eloped to Brooke County, West Virginia in 1935.

Smiley & Jimmy Gallippi elope & marry on November 30, 1935

Gina & Adam Scarano marry in 1936

Virginia, who wanted to be called 'Gina', followed suit when she and **Adam Scarano** *(born 1911)* secretly eloped. They drove to Brooke County, West Virginia and were married in October of 1936. The next day the couple felt guilty for excluding their family from the wedding and decided to repeat the ceremony at Our Lady Help of

Christian Church in November of 1936. Gina later confessed to her niece she and Adam lived separately, pretending the first marriage in West Virginia never took place.

Tony & Kay Gallippi in November 1936

Rose & Bill Jubic in 1936

Rose married **Bill Jubic** *(born 1918)* in 1936; and, Tony and Kay Gaetano married in November of 1936.

Tony and Kay's romance began when they attended a dance at Kingsley House. The 29-year-old Tony saw 21-year-old Kay and asked her to dance. Kay knew who Tony was; but, he didn't know who she was. When the two families lived side by side on Meadow Street, she was 11-years-old and he was 20. The romance is documented in a letter Tony's sister Mimi wrote to Kay many years later on her birthday. The letter read, *"I remember the day when Rose, Gina and I were sitting around the kitchen table talking. Tony came in to the kitchen and asked us what we thought of Kay Gaetano. We all told Tony that was great because we liked you. Tony started dating which eventually led to your marriage. We were all glad for both of you. Tony got a good wife and we got another sister. Love Mimi"* In another letter to Kay Gina wrote, *"How fortunate we were to have a mother who taught us to live the word of love for one another reminding us that in this country (America) we didn't have*

grandparents, uncles & aunts or cousins. We only had each other...
Happy Birthday. Love Gina."

Those who had married earlier began having children. Anna Gallippi and Frank Caschera's first child, **Antonina** was born, became ill and died within a year of her birth in 1930. Their son **Joseph** was born in 1931. In 1936, Jimmy & Smiley had their first son, **Joseph.** In 1937, **Ross** was born to Gina and Adam. Also in 1937, Tony and Kay's first child, **Kathleen** was still born. She was buried in Mt. Carmel Cemetery in the same grave plot as her Grandpa Giuseppe. Happiness came to Tony and Kay with the birth of their daughter **Janet** in 1938. In 1939, **Michael** was born to Jimmy and Smiley. The family had expanded.

The Gaetano's and Gallippi's in the War Years

The 1940's were influenced by WWII in the Village as elsewhere. The war brought families and community together. Sons were drafted to fight abroad and many daughters enlisted to serve their country. Tony, Mike and Bruno Gaetano were drafted into the Army and saw action in Europe and the Philippines. Mike was wounded twice in the same conflict in Italy.

Gallippi children were drawn into the conflict. Emil was drafted into the Army and Benny Gallippi enlisted in the Army after he made a decision to leave the seminary. Adeline Gallippi enlisted in the U.S. Coast Guard. Tony and Jimmy Gallippi were too old for the draft, were married and had children when America went to war. Both men worked in the steel mills during the

*July 1943 pic of Mike Gaetano, home on leave with
Mom, Rosa, after a tour of duty in Italy*

Bruno Gaetano serving as an MP on the Philippine Islands

Tony Gaetano & friend on an Army Base in 1942. Tony was a decorated war hero, honored for his heroic actions while storming Anzio Beach

war years. Pittsburgh was at the center of the *"Arsenal of Democracy"* providing steel, aluminum, munitions and machinery for the U.S., and its Allies WWII. Pittsburgh's mills contributed 95 million tons of steel to the war effort.[91]

The 1940's Brought More Family Expansion

In the 1940's, the family expanded again. There were more marriages. On the Gallippi side of the family, Emil *(known by then as Mil)* married **Anna Catherine Schafer** in 1945. The couple had arranged for Catherine to travel to Amarillo, Texas where Mil was stationed. She had never traveled before, and in the name of love for her intended, embarked on a 1,636 mile adventure, crossing 8 states... first by plane...then by train...to marry Mil Gallippi.

In a letter she wrote to her sister Marie on February 5, 1945 from Amarillo, while waiting for Mil to get the message she left for him at his camp, Catherine detailed her experiences.

Mil & Catherine married Feb. 10, 1945 in Amarillo Texas

She wrote, *"I was never afraid one moment...getting on the plane was like getting on a bus or a train."* She detailed her impressions of her first airplane ride describing the sun as *"casting a rosy red glow on the fluffy clouds"* She noted the first leg of the trip was to fly from Baltimore, her home, into Pittsburgh to connect with another plane to complete her journey. However, the flight got as far as Dayton, Ohio and was grounded due to snow. She boarded another plane that was to take her to Akron, Ohio. That plane got as far as St. Louis, MO where it landed to take on 'priority passengers', a frequent, war-time practice. She and four other women were bumped off that flight and told to take a train to Kansas City where they could transfer to another train to Amarillo. The train arrived in Amarillo late at night, and by that time, there were no available hotel rooms. However, a ticket agent helped her find a room in one of the smaller hotels. Catherine and Mil married 5 days later on February 10, 1945. After Mil was honorably discharged from the Army, the couple bought property in the Baltimore, Maryland area near Catherine's family. They built the foundation of their home, living there until they could afford to build the ranch-styled home above it, all the while raising their five children. Mil worked as a Milk Man for a local dairy, and Catherine ran a "Dutch Maid" business from home.

Benny & Theresa Gallippi in 1944

Mimi & Danny Dudash in 1945

Benny Gallippi met and married **Theresa** around 1944. Family recalls Benny seeing the tall, beautiful Theresa walking down the street and fell in love at the first sight of her. Mimi met **Danny Dudash** at a party after he was honorably discharged from the Army. For him it was love at first sight. For her, there were concerns because she was 7 years older than he. Danny knew what he wanted, and diligently pursued her until she finally said yes. The marriage lasted for more than 50 years.

The Family Continued to Expand

In 1943, **Doris** was born to Tony and Kay; & **Emil** to Gina and Adam. In 1945, **Bernadette** was born to Benny and Theresa; & **Elaine** to Mil and Catherine. In 1946, **Richard** was born to Mil and Catherine. In 1947, **Emily** was born to Rose and Bill; **Bobby** was born to Smiley and Jimmy; and **Danny, Jr.** to Mimi and Danny. That also was the year Tony & Kay's son **Joseph** died at birth and was buried next to his sister Kathleen. In 1948, two girl babies named **Gail** were born. One to Benny and Theresa, and one to Mil & Catherine. In 1949, **Joseph** was born to Mimi and Danny; and **James** to Benny and Theresa. The last four Gallippi grandchildren were born in the 1950's. **Ruth** to Mimi and Danny in 1950; **Billy** to Benny and Theresa in 1951; and twins **Karen** & **Sharon** to Mil and Catherine in 1955. The whole family mourned when Danny Jr. died suddenly in 1962 at 15-years-old. He had a heart attack one terrible evening as he returned from a school activity. Danny was buried beside his Grandpa Giuseppe, his Grandma Catarina, and his two cousins Kathleen and Joseph.

The Gallippi Family Picture Gallery

Mimi & Danny enjoy happy days with Baby Danny Jr. in 1948

Adam & Gina with Baby Ross in front of 569 Lenora St. in 1937

Jimmy holding Baby Joseph in 1936

*"(L to R) Rose holding Emily, Grandma Gallippi, Smiley
& Ross, Jimmy, Gina with Michael & Emil in front,
Baby Bobby, Danny, Mimi & Baby Danny"*

Smiley & Jimmy with Michael and Baby Bobby in 1947

Baby Doris, Kay & Janet in 1943

(L to R) Smiley, Kay, Doris, Grandma Gallippi, Joseph, Emil, Janet Bernadette, Benny & Michael in 1947

Dudash family portrait of Ruth, Danny, Joseph, Mimi and Danny Jr. in 1955

Tony with daughters Janet & Doris in 1943

Joe, Janet, Michael and Doris with Grandma in 1943

Bernadette & Gail Gallippi with cousin Bobby
on Grandma Gallippi's front stoop

Emil, Ross & Michael on Easter Sunday 1947

Mil & Catherine with their first two children
- Elaine and Baby Richard in 1946

Catherine & three children, Elaine, Richard & Gail in 1949

143

*Mil & Catherine's twin daughters Sharon &
Karen's 1st Communion in 1961*

*Children of Victoria and Nicola Martino & Antonina
& Francesco Caschera in the 1940's*

*Agnes & Roland Rogers Wedding in 1946 (L to R) Kay,
Agnes, Roland, & Kay's husband Tiny in California*

Kay and Agnes with their dad, Nick Martino in California

Agnes Martino Rogers in 1945

Joseph Caschera in 1940's

Kay Martino Groff in 1945

The Gallippi's were all about family and fun.

Posing for a picture in the back yard are Jimmy, Benny,
Adeline (Babe) and Tony Gallippi in 1944

Couples night out. Kay & Tony, Smiley & Jimmy,
family friends and Adam and Gina in 1941

Husbands invade wives Wednesday night monthly Canasta
Card Club just in time for the food to be served

Above and below are pictures of the adults annual
Halloween parties. No children were allowed.

Adeline's (Babe) Story

Adeline Carmella Gallippi, the youngest daughter of Giuseppe and Catarina, who the family called 'Babe', never married. On May 18, 1944, at age 22, Adeline enlisted as an Apprentice Seaman in the U.S. Coast Guard. She served from June 11, 1944 to July 24, 1944 on the US Coast Guard ship the *'TraSta'* in Palm Beach Florida. She returned to the Coast Guard Barracks in Washington, D.C.

on July 25, 1944 staying there until her honorable discharge on September 7, 1944 as a 'Mentally Incapacitated Veteran'. It is written in formal records, that Adeline was diagnosed with Schizophrenia. The family did not recognize Schizophrenic behavior in Adeline. They remember her as a fun-loving person and a talented artist who sketched detail drawings in charcoal. What triggered her diagnosis as she was serving on the ship for 6 weeks in 1944 is a mystery to the family that will have no answer.

It was the mid 1940's and the Veterans Administration (VA) recommended Adeline have a *'Prefrontal Lobotomy'* which was the treatment for either diagnosed or undiagnosed mental issues at that time. A VA representative came to Grandma Catarina's home on Lenora St., recommended the operation and presented the necessary papers to be signed to give permission. Without truly understanding the ramifications of the operation and following the recommendation from an authority, Grandma Catarina made her X on the line.

The treatment is a psychosurgical procedure in which the connections in the prefrontal cortex and underlying structures of the brain are severed and the brain's emotional centers at the seat of intellect are uncoupled. In the 1940's and until the end of the 1950's Lobotomy's were performed on 40,000 Americans and 10,000 Western Europeans until the results caused the practice to stop.[92]

Catarina instructed her daughter Rose to accompany Adeline on the train to the hospital where the operation was performed. That was the end of Adeline's ability to function. Her mind was altered and her wonderful artistic talent would be stifled for the rest of her life. The guilt Rose felt for taking her sister to such a fate bothered her for the rest of her life even though she could not have known what the result of the operation would be.

Adeline was moved from the hospital in Pittsburgh to a VA nursing home in Chicago and spent the next 50 years being cared for in various VA nursing homes in the Chicago area.

Adeline died at the age of 82 on December 26, 2003. The cause of her death was coronary heart disease that led to a stroke and ultimately to pneumonia. She was buried with honors that included a 3-gun salute in the Abraham Lincoln National Cemetery near Joliet, Illinois. The family was saddened by the loss of Adeline. She was a talented artist with a wonderful laugh and a tender heart.

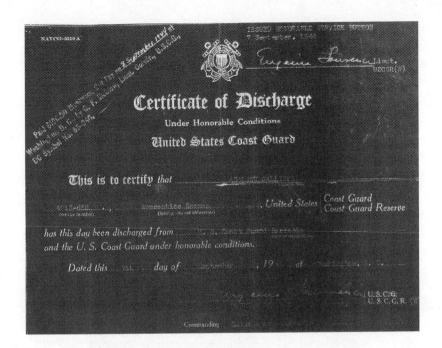

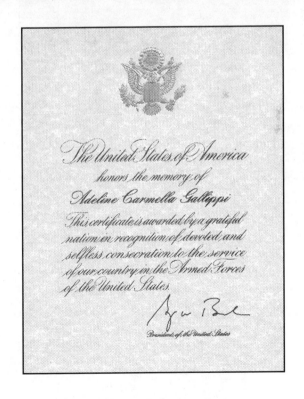

Adeline at 82 years

Adeline had a legacy she would never realize. Several months after her death, the family was notified that all the Social Security money allotted to Adeline had been kept banked in the custody of the county government who was named as her guardian. And, there was additional money from a VA insurance policy. As a result, $87,377.15 was to be distributed to her heirs. Since Adeline had 9 brothers and sisters, her estate was divided into nine equal segments. Living siblings or spouses received their entire share, and the share for siblings who had died, was distributed to their children. The irony is that the one family member who had the least, was the one who provided the most inheritance for the rest of the family. Also, it should be noted, her mother Catarina received a veteran's family disability allotment of $70 a month from 1944 until the day she died in December of 1951.

The Gaetano Side of the Family

On the Gaetano side of the family, Kay's sister Marie married **Dominic Piano** on July 25, 1945.

1946 Marie, Dom Bruno

Dominic, who was healing from a gunshot wound he sustained while fighting in the World War II Pacific Conflict, was being treated for Malaria and had just returned from New Guinea where he served under General MacArthur. The couple took a short honeymoon at Coney Island, N.Y. after which Dominic resumed treatment for Malaria at McGuire Hospital. Marie was a stunning and happy bride wearing a gown and veil handmade by her sister Kay.

Marie and Dominic's first child **Joan** was born in 1946 followed by daughters **Carol** in 1952 and **Marie** in 1958.

Pictured left is 3-year-old Joan in front of 527 Indiana Way

Pictured right is Joan & her sisters Baby Marie & Carol in 1959

Kay's brother Tony married 26-year old Ann Barbato in a 1949 gala wedding that included Kay's 6-year-old daughter Doris as the flower girl. Doris' white silk gown was handmade by Kay. Tony and Ann's children **Karen** and **Anthony** were born in the 1950's.

Kay's brother Bruno married Pearl Kammerdiener
(center couple) on February 17, 1953.

Bruno & Baby Louis in 1956

Their children are **Louis,** and twins **John** and **Rosemarie.** The birth of Bruno's first son was of particular significance to him. The child was named Louis after the man who had taken Bruno under his wing, guiding him through his fatherless childhood. Bruno's father Antonio died when Bruno was 5-years-old. He and his brothers Tony and Michael felt the loss of a father's influence in the home while being raised by their sister Catherine and their mother Rosa.

Bruno's surrogate father was known as *'Louie the Hardware Man'* because he owned and operated a large hardware store on Larimer Avenue within sight of the Gaetano home. Louie was a highly respected member of the tightly knit community. He sensed early on that Bruno had a mind for how machines and radios worked. He was curious about tools and would ask Louie how things were put together. For Bruno, being in the hardware store was like playing in a sandbox with all the toys he could have. The relationship was a natural for Louie because he was a single man with no children of his own to teach. The two bonded and when Bruno was not in school he was with Louie in the hardware store, learning.

When Bruno was 12-years-old, the time came for him to receive the sacrament of Confirmation at Our Lady Help of Christian Church. A sponsor was required and Bruno asked Louie to be his sponsor. Louie had to gently decline, explaining to Bruno that he was a Jew, and, therefore, not qualified to be a Confirmation sponsor. Bruno was heartbroken; but, Louie didn't just let the matter drop. He helped Bruno find a Catholic man in the neighborhood to sponsor him, and bought Bruno a complete suite of clothing for the occasion. He also attended the Mass in support of the boy. When we talk about the Larimer Avenue Village being a community of people who looked out for each other, we only have to look at this example to understand.

Kay's brother Michael remained single, lived with and supported his mother Rosa until her death in 1970. He worked in and around the Pittsburgh community until his death in 1972.

Michael Gaetano in the late 1960's

Gaetano Grandchildren

*Kay & Tony with Bruno and Pearl's twins John
and Rosemarie, and big brother Louis*

*A 1958 Christmas gathering of the Gaetano family
enjoying each other in Monroeville*

CHAPTER 7

DORIS' CHILDHOOD RECOLLECTIONS

In previous chapters, the story of the voyagers and their offspring was told from a historic perspective, using known facts, documented history, family recollections and some imagination to understand their experiences. We sailed with them as they made their way from Italy to America and learned of the families' adaptation to living in a new country.

This portion of the story is being told first hand since my life began in the Larimer Avenue Village. As previously stated, I'm Doris, daughter of Tony and Kay, and I was born in 1943. My family lived in an apartment building at 525 Larimer Avenue across the street from the Larimer Avenue School and Labriola's Grocery Store.

Our apartment was a second-floor walk-up unit, one of the 20 apartments stacked in the 3-story building. Access to the building was gained through glass doors at the sidewalk level that opened to a wide, center hallway. At its end were tall staircases leading to each group of apartments on the second and third floors.

Our apartment was located next to Liz Calkins apartment, my sister Janet's good friend. For several years, my Uncle Benny and Aunt Theresa Gallippi, and their children, lived in the apartment across the square landing from ours. Aunt Marie had already married Dominic Piano and was living in a third floor apartment on the other side of the building.

Just inside our apartment door was a narrow hallway that led to a living room of many patterned items including the sofa, the chair, the curtains, the rug and the walls. All of the patterns had similar colors but none of the patterns matched. A small gas stove was tucked into the corner of the living room, provided the only heat for the whole apartment. Just beyond the living room was the kitchen and to its left, the bathroom. The bedroom was to the right as you entered the apartment, and my sister and I slept in its adjacent alcove. The floor of the alcove sported a faded pink and blue, fairy-tale patterned slick of linoleum. In the corner was the wardrobe that held our clothing and the 'boogie man' I was sure lived inside. Our home was typical of apartment city living in the Village at the time... small, cozy and having just enough room to meet our needs. The rent was $17 per month according to my mom's budget book.

Janet, Uncle Adam, Cousin Ross, Daddy Tony, Doris and Cousin Emil during a visit to our apartment in 1949

Janet & Doris in our parlor of many patterns

The window of our tiny kitchen faced Indiana Way, known as the alley, and the row house where my Nonni Rosa lived with uncles Tony, Mike and Bruno.

Summers were hot. The air was still most nights and no one had air conditioning. I don't even remember knowing about air conditioning. On those summer evenings everyone was trying to sit on my Nonni Rosa's porch, or her steps, or lean on her porch railing.

Back Row - Mother Kay and Uncle Dominic
Front Row - Liz Calkins, sister Janet, Doris' friend,
Doris, Cousin Joan and a neighbor's child

Porch sitting went on into the 1950's, even after the porch had to be replaced because Nonni wore out the wooden one by scrubbing it every day.

The kids played in the alley most of the time. The games were hop-scotch, or pretending to be Annie Oakley and getting tied to a telephone pole. The goal was to get our six-guns out of their holsters to kill the bad guys so our friends could rescue us. As soon as the street lights went on, all the kids shouted, *"First American Street Light!"* It was a ritual. To this day, I don't know why we shouted except maybe the game was about who could yell it first. The penetrating heat encouraged my dad to take my hand and walk to Moio's to get a lemon ice to cool us off. Sometimes my mom and sister would go with us and we would bring back a cardboard carrier holding cone-shaped paper cups filled with lemon ice to cool off my grandmother, cousins or whoever was hanging around her porch that night. That lemon ice must have been nearly as cold as dry ice because it would take forever for the darn stuff to melt. And, I would always get "brain freeze" from eating it too quickly with those flat, little wooden spoons. I remember fighting to stay outside as long as I could so I would not have to go up to our hot apartment with fans whirring all night.

Summer days were spent in our bathing suits in the alley being hosed down to stay cool. Sometimes we had buckets of water to throw on ourselves. Mother always made us wear those tacky, white rubber bathing caps secured with an uncomfortable chin strap. And, there were those special occasions when we swam in the Highland Park pool.

Sister Janet cooling off with neighborhood kids

163

On some evenings we would drive to Highland Park and lay on a blanket on the grass. There always seemed to be a cool breeze there and picking out the constellations was fun. There was more than one night when the whole family fell asleep on the blanket, woke up at 2 in the morning and piled in the car for the ride home.

Family Gatherings & Family Stories

Family gatherings were held at either Nonni Rosa or Nonni Catarina's house. Their homes seemed to be the center of activity no matter where everyone else lived. There were savory thanksgiving dinners in Nonni Catarina's kitchen. The adults sat around the huge table in the center of the room and the kids were tucked in around the 'kids table' off to the side of the kitchen. Our turkey dinners were not typically American in design. Home-made spaghetti, served in the place of stuffing, an assortment of vegetables cooked Italian-style and that wonderful chicken soup were on our table. There was no corn, cranberry sauce, apple sauce, coleslaw or waldorf salad on our tables. All foods were Italian even at other occasions. For that matter, I don't remember eating peanut butter until I was 14-years-old.

The Stories

Occasionally, one of my aunts would do a little reminiscing about their childhood in that kitchen. Aunt Gina enjoyed telling the story about how she and her siblings were required to take turns sitting in the chair to the right of Nonni Catarina. If anyone else at the table misbehaved, Nonni would slap the child sitting next to her. She remembers my dad gathering his sisters and brothers before dinner telling them he would get even with them if they misbehaved because it was his turn to sit beside *'Mom'*.

I understand she had many tricks to control the behavior of so many children. Also, the disciplinary tool of choice was the brush side of the broom. Stories of its application were frequent lore for us children. One story centered on my aunts, who as teenagers, were smoking and hanging out of the third floor window so the smoke would not be detected in the house. Nonni, who didn't miss a thing, sat on a chair at the bottom of the stairs, broom in hand, yelling at them for smoking. In Italian she would say, *"You have to come down sometime. I'll be waiting."*

My mother, Kay tells a similar story about Nonni Rosa waiting behind the front door with broom in hand for her because she was late coming home from a date with a young man when she was 19.

Kay knew her mother was there and reached her hand inside the door grabbing her mother's hand to keep from being swatted while she smiled and said good night to her date.

During my childhood I remember Nonni Rosa being very picky about cleanliness in her house. She would lay newspapers on the floor beginning at the front door and along the path through the living room to the kitchen. On rainy days, my wet shoes would stick to the newspaper that would come up with every step. I would spend some time extricating myself from what came to be known as *'the newspaper trap'*. Of course, there were layers of slipcovers on the sofa and anywhere a person would sit.

She like to layer things, like her clothing. She was a short woman with a 50" waist line when I was a child. She would dress first in her boxer-styled underwear and a corset-type bra over which she would put an undershirt, then a slip, then her dress, then her full wrap-around apron and then a sweater or vest of some sort. All of this hung over tan cotton stockings and mid-heeled black oxfords that laced up in the front.

Sisters sitting in Nonni's house with our feet on the newspaper

165

Every one of her grandchildren remembers what happened when they entered Nonni's house. She would grab our wrists and lead us to the kitchen sink to wash our hands before we touched anything. Cousin Carol remembers this clearly as well as the *'modesty rule'*. If Carol was sitting in Nonni's kitchen wearing bermuda shorts, a tea towel would be quickly placed across her bare knees.

Nonni in her kitchen with my dad Tony after church on Sunday

Nonni always had a selection of food she cooked and placed in bowls topped with flat dishes on top of her kitchen gas heater. Sundays, directly after church, we would go to her house for our second breakfast which my father never failed to enjoy. For me, Sundays were the best because I could smell simmering spaghetti sauce as I passed the houses in the alley. Sundays were all about the traditional, the afternoon meal and family gatherings.

The Village was a Lively Place

Larimer Avenue was always bustling. My dad operated his construction business "Gallippi Home Builders" in a store front space beside our apartment building. He was accessible most of the time and mother was our stay-at-home mom who occasionally took in sewing, using her tailoring skills to make a few dollars. Mom continued to spend some of her time caring for her mother.

Mom and Dad with Nonni

*Tony and his accountant, Mr. Cifers above,
and working in his shop below.*

Neither the Depression of the 30's nor the war years and post war years of the 40's and early 50's, hampered the energized inhabitants of the Larimer Avenue Village. The two grandmothers, Rosa and Catarina, were involved with their children who either lived in their homes or a block or two away. Uncle Jimmy and his family lived upstairs in Nonni Catarina's house for a couple of years before they bought their first home on Dean Street located just beyond the Larimer Avenue Bridge. Aunt Rose and Uncle Bill lived there for a time as well. Aunt Rose was comforted by the closeness of her mother when her first child, a boy, was born prematurely at five months and died on April 28, 1940. His name was William Jubic Jr.

Larimer Avenue School was across the street from our apartment building and Jenny, our crossing guard, greeted us every morning and afternoon as she stopped traffic on the avenue so we could cross. The old school was a grand building in the eyes of this little girl, just as it was for her grandfather who witnessed its completion in 1896. There were wide, black stone steps leading to a platform that fronted the school's tall entrance doors. The doors were set into an impressive archway adorned with a bas relief of Romanesque figures 'at the seat of learning'. On the inside, the floors and stairs were made of white marble, worn in places of heavy traffic. A highly-polished brass banister bordered the stairs to the upper floors.

In the entrance, children were greeted by auspicious bronze busts of George Washington and Abraham Lincoln flanked by American Flags attached to brass flag poles. I felt I was entering an important place. To me it was like the gateway to America. The basement level of the building was reserved for kindergarten children. The first floor housed the Principal's office, the auditorium added in 1904, and first through third grade classrooms. The upper floor was for the fourth, fifth and sixth graders and the gymnasium that was added in 1931. The gymnasium was the exclusive domain of Miss Erwin, a former member of the Women's' Air Corps (WAC). There was no mistaking who was in charge. It was Miss Erwin in her tan skirt, heavy cloth stockings, oxford shoes and a whistle that hung around her neck at all times.

The school Principal, Dr. Bernice L. Storey, and all the teachers were single, white women. Among them were Miss Smith, who taught kindergarten; and Miss Cataula who taught 4th grade. The only man on staff was the janitor, Mr. Twiddle. Miss Cataula is remembered for being a high-fashioned eccentric who kept a pile of colorful, spike-heeled shoes at the bottom of her supply closet. Her 'class pets' were allowed to dust her shoes with a feather duster as an honored treat. I had the pleasure only once.

The School Yard had a variety of swings, a see-saw and was surrounded by a high, black wrought iron fence kids would rake sticks against as they walked by. Organized activities were held in the yard during summer break. One event seared in my memory happened in the summer of my 6th year of life. It was the talent show. My mother, who was heavily involved in the Parent Teacher's Association, thought it would be great for me to sing a song and dance to a tune from a movie of the time while carrying a baby doll dressed in the same outfit I would wear...a purple fringed skirt and a yellow fringed shirt with a large, yellow bow clipped to the back of my long, black curly locks. She made the matching outfits and I performed the song and dance with the doll on the platform in front of those tall doors to the school. The song went like this *"Oh you beautiful doll, you great big beautiful doll. Let me put my arms around you. I could never live without you. If you ever leave me how* *my heart would ache, I want to love you, but I feel you'd break, Oh... Oh... Oh... Oh... Oh, you beautiful doll"*. Sorry to present the burden of these lyrics; however, it has helped me exorcise the terror of performing in front of people at 6 years old. No Shirley Temple was I.

The Club Yard across the street from our school and at the end of the alley was for bike riding, baseball and those wonderful, Saturday night band performances that followed the saints' day statue parade in the streets. More than once I dressed in my white communion dress, veil and all, and carried a white gladiola while parading with my sister communicants through neighborhood streets so people could pin dollars on the saints' sashes.

Going Upstreet *(what we called the large shopping district of East Liberty)* on the #6 streetcar to see a Saturday afternoon movie was a common activity. It would cost 10 cents for the streetcar (5 cents each way), 10 cents for the movie and a nickel for popcorn or a box of liquorish pieces, or milk duds. If you wanted a Clark Bar or Hershey Chocolate Bar. Big decisions were made at the refreshment counter. Once you took your seat, being careful not to sit on one that had chewing gum on the edge, the *"Flash Gordon"* serial would begin followed by a short *"Movietone"* feature and the cartoon. Then the main movie would begin. It could be a tame adventure about *"Lassie"* or a scary movie like *"The Thing"* or *"The Creature from the Black Lagoon"*. We really didn't care what the movie was... it was a movie on a big screen and we were with our cousins to have fun. Movies were a special treat because our entertainment usually came in the form of sound from the radio at home, or from our Uncle Jimmy strumming on the guitar, leading a family sing along in these pre-television times.

Mom would take me upstreet for my tap and ballet dance lessons at the Gene Kelly Dancing Studio. The ballet was to make me more graceful, and taking formal tap dancing lessons was to encourage me to take the ballet lessons. I loved to tap dance and did it frequently, everywhere I could. All was going well until, when practicing in our second floor apartment, I dislodged a ceiling light in the apartment directly below. That pretty much ended the dancing lessons.

No matter what the activity when we were upstreet, we *always* went to Woolworth's 5 & 10 to have lunch at their lunch counter. The lunch was *always* grilled cheese and a lemon blend. I don't remember being allowed to order anything other than that. Once I bought my mom some 'Blue Waltz Perfume' for her birthday at that 5 & 10. I thought it was great because I liked the shape and color of the bottle. What I didn't know was it was the favorite perfume of women of the street at that time. I guess mom didn't know that either, until I presented it to her and she opened it during her monthly Canasta Card Club gathering at our house. For the 8 women sitting around our kitchen table, the scent became the event of the evening.

Street Entertainment

In the 40's, *'hucksters'* were still plying their wares through the streets of the Village. I could hear *"pepperoli, pepperoli, pepperoli"* being sung out as one would approach our street. I could see my Nonni Rosa and the village women walking to the huckster's open wagon with their hands in the pockets of their aprons reaching for those small leather change purses they carried with them. There was dickering over the price until the poor man realized he would lose many sales from this gang of matrons

The Matrons...Mrs. Zacardi, Mrs. Iacurchi & Nonni Rosa

holding change if he didn't comply with their desire to pay just so much for a pepper, an onion, a tomato, or several carrots bound together.

The *'Ice Man'* could be seen still servicing some who had ice boxes in their kitchens, and the *'Rag Man'* would come through occasionally to try to collect old cloth from anyone who had some they didn't want.

Then there were those visits from *'The Pony Man'*, who for a few cents would give a child a ride on his pony. I don't remember being thrilled by the experience; but, my family thought it was pretty cool. In later years, my Uncle Mil was surprised to know I also had the pony ride experience since his happened in 1922 and mine in 1947. *(See his picture on page 91)*

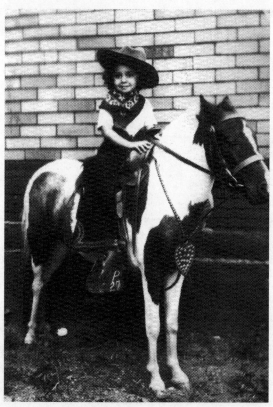

Doris on the Pony at 4-years-old

My favorite street entertainment came from Pasquale Patricca, *'The Poll Parrot Man'*, whose handcart carried a large wooden case of small drawers each containing a fortune. For a penny, *'Polly'*, the parrot, would pick a drawer, open it and pull out a very small rolled up paper fortune that it would drop in my hand. What a thrill! It was all about being so close to the parrot, not the fortune because I don't think any of us were reading well enough at 5 or 6 years old to know what was written on that small piece of paper.

The picture of Mr. Patricca, Polly and a little girl is from a June 22, 2005 edition of "Gateway Newspapers" that featured the article "Larimer Avenue as the Forerunner of East Suburbs" on page B-1 of the "Neighbor's" section.

The Church

The Catholic Church continued to be ever present in our lives. Of course there was church on Sunday mornings and the parade of neighbors walking up Meadow Street to Our Lady of Help Christian Church, and down Larimer Avenue to Sts. Peter and Paul Church to attend Mass on holy days of obligation.

Ethnic church preferences were not as important in the 1940's and 1950's as they were in the community's early days. Importance rested only on getting to Mass. Receiving the sacrament of Baptism,

Holy Community or Confirmation were a cause for religious and familial celebration.

Doris & Sister Communicants at their First Communion in the late 1940's

Janet's First Communion in the early 1940's

Cousin Emily's First Communion in the 1950's

Catechism was held after school during the week for those of us who were not attending Catholic school. Walking home along Meadow Street on those shortened fall days was always a treat because the street was filled with tons of leaves I could crunch under my feet and kick in the air. At the end of that walk was our warm apartment filled with my family sitting by steam covered windows in the kitchen. The aroma of Mom's fresh-cooked beef soup filled the air. It smelled so good. It smelled like home.

Raised by a Village

I had a happy childhood, surrounded by witty and musical people who would break out in song at the slightest provocation. I felt like I was related to everyone in the neighborhood. My relatives and Godparents were everywhere, watching every move every kid made. If you weren't related to the person standing next to you, someone in the neighborhood was.

Uncle Tony with Doris and Janet in 1945

Catherine, Janet, Tony,Balt Ellaine?, Doris 1950

Nonni Gallippi, Janet, Dad, Cousin Elaine, her dolly and Doris in 1949

Mom & Dad talking with a neighbor in front of 525 Larimer Avenue

Sometimes everyone looking out for everyone else would come in handy, like the day I got myself in trouble. As a 6-year-old, I decided to take a ride on the clothesline suspended between our building and the building across the alley that was threaded through a pulley-system. I had watched my mother swing our wash out to dry on that clothesline many times. I leaned out the kitchen window, grabbed the rope and immediately swung to the center of the alley. I remember my mother coming to the window, shaking her hand at me and screaming. In very emotional Italian she said, "Doris 'vieni qua' *(come here)"* and something about killing me if I didn't. *(Making that specific threat in Italian was frequently used by frustrated mothers in my neighborhood to get children to behave. They never really meant it, of course, but when they said it we knew we were in big trouble.)* I remember thinking it might be better to let go and fall than to try to reunite with my mother. I could see my father in the corner of my eye pushing my mother away from the window as he clearly felt she was not being helpful. I remember he tried to pull the clothesline back toward our building and the movement scaring me. That's when he stopped. The memory of how, or who got me down is blocked; but, I didn't fall. I was most likely rescued by one of the neighbors. I was a curious kid, and the one who accidently got her tongue stuck to a metal pole one freezing winter because I wanted to see what ice tasted like. It became painfully clear my mother was not prepared to deal with a kid like me after raising my well-behaved, neat and orderly, older sister. After mom freed me by pouring a pot of warm water over my tongue and prying it from the metal pole, I was punished for upsetting her.

Family Gatherings

As city folk the family looked for opportunities to get out in the open air. Once a year the entire clan made its way to *"Twin Willows"*, a park on the outskirts of Pittsburgh with picnic tables, a wooden dance floor under a center pavilion and a swimming pool. It was all about having fun and there were practically no limits on it. Other picnickers were drawn to the enticing aromas of the food cooking on our open grill. There sat a tray of pasta and spaghetti sauce; a pot of sausage, peppers and onions; premade 'porpettes', a meatball mixture formed into oblong, bite size pieces for easy eating *(instead of plain hamburgers);* 'rice patties' and 'frittatas' (eggs scrambled with peppers, cheese and sausage). There was the occasional hot dog placed on the grill as my dad just loved the things. We never had regular picnic foods, except for that occasional hot dog that mysteriously showed up. We may have been in America but our foods were always Italian. The main meal was topped off with Aunt Mimi's chocolate cake, Aunt Smiley's pineapple squares and 'The Watermelon'. Uncle Adam and I would plot our attempt to get the edge on each other for that traditional watermelon face wash. I was no match for him, for sure but he allowed me to win sometimes.

The Gallippi family at one of our many picnics pictured above, and another pictured below. There seemed to be no end to the fun.

When one family member would suggest an activity, the whole family would jump in. There were those picnics, swimming in Highland Park, and trips to *'Geneva on the Lake'* and Atlantic City, NJ. Also, there were annual trips to Lake Erie for a swim in the Lake.

Aunt Marie at Lake Erie

Aunt Gina at Geneva on the Lake

We'd spend a night in a cabin and picked black cherries from the nearby orchards. We climbed ladders propped against the trees. For every cherry that made it into the container, one went into the mouth. I remember my 'Honest Abe' dad giving the orchard owner a few extra bucks to cover our filching. Lake Erie was polluted at the time with oil slicks from the ships. The Lake had nearly died by then and few fish were surviving. After swimming, our feet would be coated with black oil and the family decided the best solution would be to wear white rubber bathing shoes. The whole family bought them at Mr. Alan's 5 & 10 store on Larimer Avenue and wore them at the next outing. What a sight.

Sometimes the activities were strictly for adults. There was the Wednesday night, monthly Canasta Club where the women played cards and gossiped and the husbands showed up just about the time the food was being served. The women complained saying it was their night out but the men just showed up to eat anyway.

There were those infamous Halloween parties our parents would have. We only learned of their highball drinking fun when we, as adults, found old black and white pictures of them.

Lillian Home Camp, sponsored by the Kinsley House, provided a different experience for us. The children spent two weeks at the camp in the summer enjoying outdoor activities that included swimming and crafts. We slept in cabins, took cool showers outside and listened to stories around a campfire at night. One mother would volunteered to attend with us and it was mostly Aunt Marie. I remember it not being my favorite place because I didn't like the food and I would be covered with mosquito bites when we returned home. Maybe that's where my idea of being in the great outdoors formulated. I now prefer sitting in a comfortable chair on a screened-in porch, eight feet off the ground. After 1952, when the family moved from the city, reunions were held as another excuse to have fun. They took on a special significance as the family grew older and lived in different parts of the United States.

Maria Catarina Gallippi at 72-years-old

Nonni Catarina Dies

It was a sad time when an icon of our family, our Nonni Catarina, died at 72 on July 23, 1951. She had a stroke and lingered for several weeks. I was 8-years-old at the time and realized I would not have her welcoming arms around me anymore. The family gathered at La Rosa's Funeral Home to say our last goodbyes. In those days, when a person died, the custom was to have three days of open coffin visitations at the funeral home before a solemn Mass of Christian Burial was held at Our Lady Help of Christian Church.

Nonni had lived in the Larimer Avenue Village for 45 years and had dozens of friends. Many strangers she had helped and fed at her door through the years came to pay their respects to a woman who genuinely cared about everyone around her. On the morning of the last day of the viewing, the family lined up, passed the coffin touching her, and for some, kissing her which was the custom.

CHAPTER 8

THE BEGINNING OF THE END OF THE ITALIAN VILLAGE

The old style Larimer Avenue Village began to unravel as the Italian speaking immigrants aged, and a new wave of opportunities became available for their children outside of the community. The same was occurring with the neighboring Polish community. Coinciding with the families' evolution was the launching of Pittsburgh's clean air and civic revitalization project called *"The Renaissance"*. It began in 1946 following WWII. The intent of Pittsburgh's politicians was to clean up the infamously sooty Pittsburgh air and to expand industrial businesses; thereby, increasing the economic base of the city. East Liberty and the Larimer Avenue Village were the first of many victims of a failed urban renewal project called the *"Title I Housing Act of 1949"*. Initially, this Act sanctioned the demolition of vast swaths of buildings in Pittsburgh where the Monongahela and Allegheny Rivers met the Ohio River at what was known as *"The Point"*. During the second phase, 95 acres of the Lower Hill District area inhabited by African Americans was completely destroyed through an act of eminent domain and the City took ownership. As a result, hundreds of small businesses and more than 8,000 people were forcibly dispersed. The idea was to clear the land to build a cultural center that included a civic arena. The civic arena was built but only one other building for the center was erected. The project came to a standstill and was never finished.[93]

With no planning for where these very poor 1,239 black families and 312 white families would go, the displaced families were on their own to find housing. They moved into surrounding, low-cost neighboring areas one of which was the Larimer Avenue Village. The Village was attractive because it provided a safe, well-structured neighborhood with established families, schools, transportation, businesses and decent housing. They could live cheaply. The cost of an apartment our size at that time was about $18 a month. Hundreds of families arrived in the Village crowding schools and residents. They were considered 'invaders' in this exclusively Italian neighborhood.

One can't deny there was resentment and prejudice. African Americans were not only judged by the color of their skin; but, for their reputation of being unskilled and underemployed. Since they didn't speak Italian, building neighborly relations with the people who were established in the community was difficult. Resentment was not spoken of publicly. It was low-key, hovering under a public politeness that existed between the groups. It doesn't seem enough to give this issue a slight reference; however, this story is to tell of my families' extraordinary journey and evolution from Italian immigrant status. I could not presume to have answers to the incredibly complicated issue of race relations, or how those relations played out in the Village given the fact that I moved from there when I was 9-years-old. But, history gives us a window through which insight is gained. Italians elected to come to America for the opportunities this country promised. African Americans carried a legacy of being forcibly brought to America, not for their personal opportunities; but, for the opportunities of others. The discrimination Italians experienced, while not to be shortchanged, pales in comparison to the African American experience.

When my family began to emigrate from Italy in the late 1800's, slavery had been 'officially' abolished, worldwide. But, segregation still existed in America's Jim Crow south. Racism reared its ugly head from generation to generation keeping African Americans psychologically and socially down. As a result, in 1915-16, African Americans began a great migration from southern America to urban environments in the north. "The growing urban trend of race discrimination began. Regardless of the cause, whether deep-seated fears, competition for jobs and neighborhoods, or simply ignorance, blacks in all (northern) cities were excluded from industrial work, labor unions, certain skilled occupations, and white-collar work. No matter where they started, by 1920, they were overwhelmingly overrepresented in semiskilled/unskilled work." Upward movement was nearly impossible.[94]

Emigrating Italians had choices and were selective when choosing the city they felt would work for them. Mostly decisions were based on a "village-chain migration pattern".[95] "The types of skills Italians brought to America, or could acquire through kin assistance, were in demand in most American communities. The process of city building required masons, carpenters and bricklayers as well as railroad and public works laborers."[96] Italians were more successful at transforming these opportunities into satisfactory blue-collar or even lower level white-collar work.[97]

The combination of what was seen as the 'invasion' of the Italian sanctuary, and the development of Pittsburgh suburbs, became the perfect storm for the exodus of Italians from the Larimer Avenue Village. (Autos with long distance capability were affordable and were purchased by young families). President Eisenhower spearheaded the construction of the Pennsylvania Turnpike that would bring eastern and western Pennsylvania (PA) together and would connect PA to the State of Ohio. While some families were moving to Pittsburgh's Frankstown Road area, my father saw the future in a community 11 miles west of Pittsburgh where Exit 6 of the PA Turnpike was being built. The borough was called Monroeville, and land was available for purchase.

Our first car parked on Larimer Avenue.
This car drove us to Monroeville

My Dad, Tony Gallippi, standing on the western extension of the PA Turnpike in the spring of 1951 before it opened. This section would connect Pennsylvania to Ohio by November of 1951.

My dad, as the oldest male in his family, took the lead for the family and arranged for the purchase of Mr. Shackleford's Flower Farm, a tract of land located on the old William Penn Highway, Route 22. He encouraged his brothers and sisters, and my mother's brother, to build new homes on the hill of what was a flower farm.

My dad was the contractor of record and the agreement was that each family would help build the others' homes. His family was made up of tradesmen...several skilled carpenters; a marble setting craftsman; an electrician; and my dad, a plasterer with a design/ architectural education, who had the expertise to pull it off. Even the kids helped out. I remember my dad giving me a small bucket of 10 penny nails and a hammer telling me to start nailing the subfloor of our new home.

Tony, Kay & Doris standing on the lot where their suburban home will be built in September of 1951

First two homes built in Monroeville on Williamsburg Drive in 1952

The back of our Monroeville home while under construction

Uncle Jimmy, and sons Joe and Michael building
their home on Williamsburg Drive

When we moved to Monroeville in 1952, I had just finished the 4th grade in the Larimer Avenue School. My life changed dramatically. Monroeville at the time was not commercially developed. It was open land dotted with corn fields and dairy farms, and inhabited by white, Anglo-Saxon Protestants. Imagine the shock of the natives when they saw this band of dark-haired, good-natured Italians, with song in their hearts and hope in their future romping all over their territory. We were the "invaders" who moved into their neighborhood. We were truly 'city-folk' and that was never more evident than when the family tried to have a corn roast. We gathered on one of my father's vacant lots on the hill to build a bonfire and discovered no one knew a thing about how to start a fire. A frustrated Uncle Jimmy bellowed, *"Bring me a farmer!"* and dispatched my cousin Joe to find a neighbor to help. He found a neighbor who was kind enough to come over and get the fire started. Our new neighbor and his family were invited to join us and did as Uncle Jimmy strummed his guitar and we all sang. After that, everything seemed to be alright. The prejudice against us didn't last long. It was probably because we were landowners living in finely crafted, individual homes. All heads of households had jobs and the children were well-behaved. Only one family felt it necessary to move from the area. It was the family who owned the lovely old mini-mansion on two, iron-gated acres next to our new ranch-styled home. The very blond home owner, a mattress salesman, never hesitated to show his disdain, and felt it would be better for his family to move to Ohio before the neighborhood went to pot.

At 9-years-old the move to Monroeville put me in culture shock. In the Larimer Avenue Village every shopkeeper and everyone's grandmother spoke Italian. English was rarely heard on the streets or in the homes. In Monroeville, everyone spoke English and I was really surprised the first time I heard my new girlfriend's grandmother speak English.

And, then there was the environment itself. Monroeville was open country with grass and trees. I was accustomed to living near tightly-fit buildings arranged on narrow streets and the smell of wet cement sidewalks on rainy days. We had moved from our small city apartment to a three-bedroom, 2-bathroom rambling home, complete with a large office for my dad and located on a half an acre of land.

The house had an upstairs space large enough to make an apartment for my Uncle Bruno and his new wife Pearl to live in during the first year of their marriage.

There was another cultural change. All my new friends played different games. They liked to 'playact' in their made to order playhouses above their garages when my idea of having fun was sifting dirt in the Club Yard with old discarded window screens, or skipping rope, or being a rescued cowgirl.

Since Monroeville was not developed enough to accommodate the influx of city people, the little Monroeville elementary school could not accommodate all the additional students. My cousin Emil and I were bussed to Wilmerding for 5th grade and then to Wilkinsburg for 6th grade before a Junior High School was built just up the road from our house on old William Penn Highway. There was no high school either. My sister and cousins Joe, Mike and Ross traveled to the adjacent town of Turtle Creek for their high school years. By the time I was ready for high school, the Gateway Regional Senior High School had been built and 1,000 high school aged children from the very small towns of Turtle Creek, Pitcairn, Wall, Wilmerding and Monroeville attended that school.

The final phase of our families Americanization began once the majority of our family settled in suburban Monroeville and the balance settled in other surrounding communities. My mother, like other mothers of the time, got a job in the mid 1950's. She used her magnificent sewing skills to secure a job in the Alteration Department of the newly constructed J.C. Penney store at the "Miracle Mile", the first strip shopping center in Monroeville. She really liked that job. She worked there until 1983; and, especially liked the group of friends she made in our new community.

My Father continued to operate his building business. After the 17 homes were built on Williamsburg Drive, he partnered with other builders to build homes in surrounding Pittsburgh suburbs but the recession in the early 1950's ground the nation's economy to a halt. The homes he built on speculation did not sell causing him to declare bankruptcy to help put our family's finances back on track. I remember the feelings of defeat in my father and how my mother's salary at J.C. Penney's was the only money coming into the household. I have to say we never went without a meal during the time it took to work themselves out of it. My dad went back to working at plastering which was his original trade and continued to plaster throughout the balance of his career until he retired at 65-years-old. All was not dark though, my dad as a skilled, master plasterer, was called

Ad in Pittsburgh newspaper for homes Tony Gallippi built

upon to do specialized jobs like the plaster ornamentation in Jacquelyn Kennedy Onassis' apartment in New York City, and the expansive lobby ceiling of the Rayburn Office Building in Washington, D.C. He said while working on the Washington job, he felt like Michael Angelo lying on his back on a scaffold near the ceiling as he plied his craft. After nearly a year of working on the ceiling, he and his partner decided to sign their creation in plaster.

In the true spirit of his adventurous and creative nature, my dad began to study oil painting and cultivated his art studying color throughout his retirement years. Many of his creations coupled his architectural skills with his new-found study of color. His paintings are hanging in the homes of his children, grandchildren, nieces and nephews.

"The Yellow Taxi", a 22"x23" oil painting by Tony Gallippi

"A Bridge in Pittsburgh" a 16"x20" oil painting by Tony Gallippi

Nonni Rosa Dies at 82

While Monroeville was growing and prospering, the Larimer Avenue Village and its surrounding communities continued to degrade. In the late 1960's the family tried to convince Nonni Rosa to move to Monroeville with Uncle Michael to be near our family but she was afraid of the change and would not move. Again, the tide of history was against her as the neighborhood deteriorated to a point where it was not safe for her and Uncle Michael to continue to reside in their rowhome on Indiana Way. The Larimer Avenue Village was being destroyed by drug gangs and all the violence that goes with it. My dad investigated and subsequently secured an apartment for her and Uncle Michael in the new, low-income buildings erected as part of East Liberty's reconstruction. Rosa would not cooperate and had to be physically moved to her new apartment while my mother arranged her furniture and other household items there. By that time her health was failing, as was my Uncle Michael's. My mother made almost daily trips to East Liberty from Monroeville to see to their needs.

On the day of Nonni Rosa's death, she told Uncle Michael she was not feeling well and asked him to call a cab to take her to the hospital. The cabbie made the mistake of taking the pair on a circuitous route and when Uncle Michael attempted to tell the cabbie to take a more direct route, Nonni Rosa stopped him. She had decided she would handle this problem herself. They eventually arrived at the hospital, whereupon Rosa leaned forward, smacked the cabbie on the back of the head, chastised him for cheating a dying woman and instructed Uncle Michael not to pay the fare. She entered the hospital and died of heart failure at the age of 82 on July 30, 1970.

Rosa Gaetano at 82 years old

About a year after Nonni's death, the effects of the bad gene Uncle Michael had inherited from his father became very obvious as he gradually drifted into a catatonic state. He died in 1972.

Larimer Avenue Village is no more

Today there is nothing left of the village that housed my family and so many 'new Americans' for over 100 years. On a recent visit, I was heartsick to see the destruction. Larimer Avenue was an abandoned road as far as the eye could see with broken macadam and weeds growing through it. Except for the boarded up St. Peter & Paul Church, our old apartment building at 525 Larimer, the boarded up Larimer school and the broken down building that once housed Labriola's Grocery story, there was nothing but weeds. On Indiana Way, the row of homes where my Nonni Rosa lived had been leveled as was the row behind hers and the row behind that. Nonni Catarina's house on Lenora Street had been burned to the ground by vandals and any home left standing was boarded up and condemned. A few blocks away in one direction stood the abandoned Our Lady Help of Christian Church. There was an eerie silence as I stood in the middle of the Avenue in what could no longer be anybody's home town.

Picture from abandonedonline.net/Larimer School

The Abandoned Larimer Avenue School.

The building that once housed Labriola's Grocery Store Pictures, courtesy of Peter M. Goda, Sr.

A former Larimer Avenue shop.

Indiana Way alley behind 525 Larimer Avenue in front of our Nonni Rosa's house where we played as children.

The empty corner lot upon which my Nonni Rosa's townhouse was and the continuation of the alley to the homes that were behind hers.

CHAPTER 9

THE 1960'S AND BEYOND

Family life was comfortable in the suburbs. By the early 1960's, children of the first generation Americans had graduated from high school, were in college, or already working in their chosen professions.

The Gallippi Family Buys A Country Estate

I don't know how the idea started but the family decided it needed a country estate where all could gather on the weekends and for special events. As a group they purchased a 77-acre farm in the Laurel Mountains of Pennsylvania a few miles from the Ligonier Exit of the PA Turnpike. John Kennedy was President of the United States at the time giving Uncle Jimmy the rationale for the estate's chosen name. He said, "If the Kennedy's can have *'Hyannis Port'*, we'll have *'LoAnnis Port'*." The property, with its stone main house and a substantial-sized barn, was officially named *'LoAnnis Port'*. The property remained in the family for many years with many changes being made to accommodate the family's needs. A natural spring was found on the property and it was turned into a terrazzo-tiled swimming pool for all to enjoy.

The old stone house at LoAnnis Port

LoAnnis Port   1971

Richard
Maria
Ronnie
Tony
Jerry
Karen
Smiley
Sharon
Don

Adam
Kay
Virginia
Danny

The family enjoying a weekend at LoAnnis Port

The natural swimming pool

The years went by and the property was sold as the remaining older generation felt there was no longer a need to maintain '*LoAnnis Port*'. Their children were grown and settled in other parts of the country.

Opportunity had beckoned the now adult children of that first generation of Americans and they moved to pursue the jobs with the most opportunities. For some those jobs were in California, for others they were in Ohio, West Virginia, Kentucky, Idaho, Indiana, Colorado, Arizona, New York, New Jersey, Maryland and Texas; with only a few remaining in Pennsylvania. They became educators *(from elementary to college),* government employees, engineers in charge of major U.S. divisions & projects, health care providers, administrators, certified public accountants, computer experts, and business owners. One, with a BS in psychology and an MBA, became a gentleman farmer. Another became a geologist, another a writer, and four or five served in the United States military as part of their career development.

It is not an exaggeration to say their accomplishments are too many to list here. They all became contributors to society and none ran afoul of the law of the land.

The dreams of those first voyagers...the pioneers... the risk-takers...the opportunity seekers...the grandfathers who forged the path for our family...were fulfilled.

Gina's youngest son Emil Scarano in the 1960's
during his military service in Pensacola, Fla.

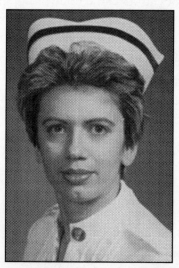

Benny's daughter Bernadette Gallippi in 1980
graduating from nursing school

Benny's son Jimmy Gallippi in 1976 during his military service

The Elders

The surviving children of Catarina and Giuseppe Gallippi, and Rosa and Antonio Gaetano grew old and began to need the assistance of their children. With encouragement, they moved to the towns where their children lived. Rose moved to California to live near her daughter Emily and her grandchild Reagan; Smiley moved to California to be near her children and grandchildren; Mimi and Danny moved to Ohio to be near their daughter Ruth and their grandchildren; Kay moved to eastern Pennsylvania to live near her daughter Doris; and Mil and Catherine moved back from Florida to live near their children in the Baltimore Maryland area. Virginia, who had moved to Florida after her husband Adam died, returned home to Pennsylvania several years later with her second husband Jack Seidman to live near her son Emil. When Jack died she continued to live near her son.

As each member of this very close family died, the others felt the loss. Of the Gallippi's, Anne died in 1981, Victoria in 1985, Tony in 1987, Jimmy in 1991 and Benny in 1999. Also Anne's husband, Frank died in 1981, Victoria's husband, Nicola died (date unknown); Jimmy's wife, Smiley died in 1999, Gina's husband, Adam Scarano died in 1990 & Benny's wife, Theresa died in the 1980's.

Tony & daughter Doris in 1987

Theresa with Benny & children Billy & Gail

Doris' daughter Nancy with her God Parents
Aunt Smiley and Uncle Jimmy in 1982

Aunt Rose with Uncle Adam as he kissed his baby
grandson Ross, Emil & Patricia's first child.

Uncle Benny with his sisters Aunt Rose, Aunt Mimi & Aunt Gina

Tony's Last Stand

My dad, Tony had a most dramatic death in August of 1987. He had gone to the new mall in Monroeville to take a picture of his niece Karen, who worked for the cosmetic company Estee Lauder at the time and was a part of a costumed feature at the store's cosmetic department. Dad lifted his camera to take the picture and his heart stopped as he clicked the shutter. He died instantly of a blood clot in his heart.

His children and grandchildren; sisters, brothers, nieces and nephews remember his good natured ways, his honesty, his generosity, his sense of justice and how he lit up a room when he entered. There was a poignant moment at his funeral mass. As we exited the church in a procession following his casket, I saw a short, very old African American man standing at the rear of the church holding his hat over his heart. Afterward, I asked my cousin Joe if he knew who the man was. Joe said when he saw the man come into the church and stand at the rear, he asked him to join the family and take a seat in a pew. Joe said the man refused saying he was there to stand in honor of "Blackie" (my dad's nickname). The old man said in the early days, when he worked with my dad as a Hod Carrier on plastering jobs, my dad always made sure he had a job so he could support his family. It's hard to think of a more moving tribute. After some 30 years, this gentleman remembered my dad's understanding of injustice. Back then, black people in Pittsburgh were not given many opportunities for work.

The funeral occasion was sad, indeed. But, on that warm August day more than the sun shined as the family gathered in the backyard of my parents' home for a luncheon after the service. Standing in front of my Aunt Mimi and Uncle Danny was their young grandson Billy. The little boy looked like their son Danny Jr. who died when he was a boy. I was struck by the likeness and looked at my aunt not quite knowing what to say. She read my mind and calmly said, "We got him back".

The 1999 Gallippi Family Reunion

In 1999, Mimi and Danny, with the help of their daughter Ruth and her husband, Dave decided to hold a family reunion held in Monroeville. It was a joyous occasion at which every living member of the older generation, and many of their children and grandchildren joined together for one big party. It was both a moving time for many of us, who had not seen our relatives in years, and an enormous surprise to see how much bigger the family had become.

(Above left to right) Rose, Mil, Catherine, Mimi, Danny, Kay & Gina

18 of the 20 First Cousins attended the Family Reunion in 1999

20 of the 22 second cousins attended the 1999 Family Reunion

Including Gillian scheduled to be born in November, 15 third cousins attended the Family Reunion in 1999.

A Generation Passes, Save One.

The last living person from the first generation of Americans in this family is Kay Gallippi who turned 101 on February 27, 2015.

All the others have gone to their rest. Of the Gallippi family, Emilio (Mil) and Adeline died in 2001; Mimi in 2008; Gina in 2009 and Rose in 2011. Mil's wife Catherine and Mimi's husband Danny have died as well as Kay's youngest brother Bruno Gaetano.

Pictures of Kay... Great Grandmother to Chelsea, Nina, Katie, Riley, Taylor, Quinn and Gillian who call her Nonni.

Kay at 99-years-old celebrating a birthday with six of her great grandchildren at Doris' house in Reading, PA.

Kay with daughter Janet, Granddaughter Linda & Great Granddaughter Gillian on Gillian's first visit to Great Grandma's house in Monroeville.

Kay pictured here with her daughter Doris on her 101st Birthday, courtesy of Peter M. Goda, Sr.

Kay on her 100th Birthday

In Conclusion - Personal Reflections

As I watched my very sad Nonni Rosa, and sensed by mother's underlying sadness, I wondered, as a child, if I was wrong to feel happy, not sad...to be curious for information and not just satisfied to believe what was said and want explanations. In this family, a child's feelings were addressed. My dad said Nonni Rosa was sad because she had no choices about how her life would be spent. He stressed that I had choices, they were being encouraged and that was why I felt happy. He said I should look forward to getting an education and a profession before I got married. He stressed how important it was to always be in charge of my life and, if I married, I should not be dependent on my husband for my financial support. He said independence would serve me all the rest of my life. This was remarkable advice from an Italian man raised in the dominant male culture of his time. Later on in life when I asked him why he advised me the way he did, he said he had seen too much injustice for women in his time and he didn't want his daughters to suffer the same fate.

The women of the family nurtured me as well. My aunts Gina and Rose, as well as Smiley's sought opportunities to impart their advice. Aunt Gina was a fancier of opera. She was a free spirit who sang and played the organ, a person who embraced the joys of life. On more than one occasion she would say, metaphorically, *"If you want to sing... SING. The world is open to you."* She always put her advice in musical terms which I found amusing. Throughout my life she would find time to write letters to me as she traveled the world. She thought of me more as her daughter than her niece because she had two sons, great sons I might add, but no daughter to bond with in the way daughters bond with their mothers.

My Aunt Rose trumpeted her advice to me one day. She said, *"Be your own person; not somebody else's."* While I don't remember the exact circumstances, I took to heart the advice. And my Aunt Smiley, who as my Godmother, would council me from time to time when we lived close to each other. She said, *"The world is changing. You have a lot of 'smarts'. Don't let anyone try to tell you not to use them."* I loved these strong women. They were my role models. I think of them often.

The legacy left to me as a product of my first generation American family is to embrace life's challenges, to envision a future beyond

211

what is evident today, to find solutions to problems and not be afraid to take calculated risks to advance forward. This is the legacy I leave for my three very bright daughters, Rosanne, Carolyn and Nancy. There are many times I wished my daughters could have shared the riches of my childhood... to have seen the world through the eyes of newly minted Americans who took charge and handled their challenges while standing with one foot in the old world and one in the new. The seeds planted during our families' reach to be Americans grew through our generation. We blossomed because of their extraordinary journey.

FOOTNOTES

1. The name Domenico has been used as Antonio's uncle in America for the purpose of this social history. The family has recalled an uncle facilitated Antonio's emigration to America and Antonio lived with him and his wife. It is known one of his uncles, named Domenico, emigrated to America, and we know of another named Vincenzo who remained in Italy.

2. Wikipedia-the free encyclopedia: http//:www.en.wikipedia.org/wiki/ Calabria.

3. *"Pomodoro. The Tomato in Italy...and My Kitchen"* The History of Tomatoes in Italian Cuisine, by Lynne Evans.

4. Hhtp://www.everyculture.com/multi/Ha-La/Italian   Americans. Html#1x222bJhY96F

5. Ibid.

6. Angelo Pellegrini, *"An immigrants Return"*. New York. Macmillian, 1952: pp. 11, 21

7. Ibid.

8. Factmonster.com

9. Ibid.

10. Ibid.

11. Ibid.

12. Bing-Italy 1800's to 1900's
    http://www.lifeinitaly.com/history/lifeduring   19th.Century.   & Facebook-Life in Italy/home/culture/history/life from 1900-1940

13. Ibid.

14. Italian American from *"Harvard Encyclopedia of American Ethnic Groups"* by Humbert Nelli.

15. Everyculture.com/multi/Ha-La/Italian Americans. Htmi#1x222bJhY96F

16. *"The Italian Immigrant Experience in America"* 1970-1920; Mangione, 25; www.yale.edu/ynhti/curiculum/units/1991/3/99.03.06

17. Ibid.

18. Bing-Italy 1800's to 1900's
    http://www.lifeinitaly.com/history/lifeduring   19th.Century.   & Facebook-Life in Italy/home/culture/history/life from 1900-1940

19. Ibid.

20. *"The Italian Immigrant Experience in America"* 1970-1920; Mangione,

25; www.yale.edu/ynhti/curiculum/units/1991/3/99.03.06

21. http://www.everyculture.com/multi/Ha-La/Italian Americans. Html#1x222bJhY96F: footnote #22 National Park Service: Castle Garden as An Immigrant Depot: 1855-1890

22. http://www.everyculture.com/multi/Ha-La/Italian Americans. Html#1x222bJhY96F: footnote #24 Vincent J. Cannato: American Passage: The History of Ellis Island. P. 50; Harper Collins (2009) ISBN 0060742739

23. Bing-Italy 1800's to 1900's
http://www.lifeinitaly.com/history/lifeduring 19th.Century. & Facebook-Life in Italy/home/culture/history/life from 1900-1940. Italian American from *"Harvard Encyclopedia of American Ethnic Groups"* by Humbert Nelli: footnote #25 New York Times: The Ellis Island Verdict: The ruling; High Court Gives New Jersey Most of Ellis Island (2)

24. http://www.citlink.net/~messineo/patria.html: National Park Service (http://www.nps.gov/stli/index.htm)

25. *"Ellis Island & Statue of Liberty"* Magazine, an American Park Network (APN) publication and part of a collection of visitor guide magazines for national parks, state parks, and wild life parks; published by Mark Mullins. APN subsidiary of the Meredith Corporation.

26. *"Ellis Island & Statue of Liberty"* Magazine *'The Immigrant Journey historical highlights'*, 1998 American Park Network, Eighth Edition, Printed by Meredith Corporation. 58

27. Ibid

28. Ibid. 59

29. Ibid.

30. Ibid. 53

31. Ibid

32. Ibid. 27

33. Ibid.

34. Ibid. 60

35. Ibid.

36. Ibid.

37. Ibid.

38. Everyculture.com/multi/Ha-La/Italian Americans. Htmi#1x222bJhY96F

39. http:// www.en.wikipedia.org/wiki/Highland Park (Pittsburgh)

40. Ibid.

41. http://www.en.wikipedia.org/w/index.ph?title=East Liberty-Pittsburgh
42. Ibid.
43. Ibid.
44. Ibid.
45. *"Lives of Their Own, Blacks, Italians & Poles in Pittsburgh, 1900-1960"*, John Bodner, Roger Simon and Michael P. Weber. 67
46. Ibid.
47. Ibid.
48. Ibid.
48. Ibid.
49. Ibid.
50. *"Larimer Avenue"* http://www.giovannibattistaveronapa just another Word Press.com site posted November 15, 2012; From the paesi d"Italia to the village of Larimer: A study of Pittsburgh's Forgotten Little Italy, 1920-1950
51. *"Cost of Food & Dry Goods 1850-1895"* Answer. Wikipedia
52. Ibid.
53. www.measuring worth.com/uscompanies/relativevalue.php
54. *"Natural Gas Discoveries in the 19th Century: The Birth of Equitable Gas Co."*
55. *"Lives of Their Own, Blacks, Italians & Poles in Pittsburgh, 1900-1960"*, John Bodner, Roger Simon and Michael P. Weber.
56. http://www.everyculture.com/multi/HaLa/ItalianAmericans. html#ixzz2bDQhyU4S- "The Wonderful Life of Angelo Massari, translated by Arthur Massolo, New York: Exposition Press, 1965: pp. 46-47)
57. *"Business Depressions and Financial Panics"*. Samuel Reznek, New York: Greenwood Press, 1968
58. Ibid.
59. Ibid.
60. Ibid. President Eliminated Income Tax.
61. *"Progressive Era"*, Wikipedia, the free encyclopedia. Redirected from *"United States Economy and Business: 1900-1909"*. The Progressive Era was a period of social activism and political reform in the United States that flourished from 1890's to the 1920's.
62. *"Larimer Avenue"* http://www.giovannibattistaverona pa just another Word Press.com site posted November 15, 2012; from the paesi d"Italia to the village of Larimer: A study of Pittsburgh's Forgotten Little Italy,

1920-1950. Recollections from the author, Doris Gallipi's childhood through the 1940 & 1950 when these traditions still existed.

63. http://kingsleyassociation.org/about/history.

64. *"US Economy-A Brief History"*, http://www.country studies.us/United States/economy. http://www.history orb.com

65. *Theodore Roosevelt Icon of The American Century"* 1998 Smithsonian Institution national Portrait Gallery Brochure

66. *"Progressive Era"*, Wikipedia, the free encyclopedia. Redirected from *"United States Economy and Business: 1900-1909"*. The Progressive Era was a period of social activism and political reform in the United States that flourished from 1890's to the 1920's.

67. Ibid.

68. http:...wikipedia *"Santos Brazil"*

69. Ibid.

70. Ibid.

71. Ibid.

72. Ibid.

73. *"The Great Migration-as seen at the port of New York (1903)"* http:.. www.gienvick.com/Immigration/Ellis Island 1903-10

74. Ibid.

75. *"The Flood From Europe - The Immigration Problem, 1903"* http://www.gjenvick.com/Immigration/Ellis Island/1903-12-theFloodFromEurope. html#ixzz2iYJCTdav; and *"Report of the Commissioner General of Immigration to the Secretary of Labor for the fiscal year ending June 30, 1914";* Washington, DC: Government Printing Office, 1914, 7, 104-7, 110. The years 1913 and 1914 refer to fiscal years ending on June 30.

76. *"The Great Migration-as seen at the port of New York (1903)"* http:.. www.gienvick.com/Immigration/Ellis Island 1903-10

77. Ibid.

78. Ibid.

79. *"Immigrants and the Steamship Steerage Rate Wars"*; htpp://www. gjenvick.com/Steerage/1904-06-16 ImmigrantsSteerageRateWaras. html#ixzz2j7oygV8T

80. Ibid.

81. wikipedia.org/wiki/ *"Pittsburgh in the 1930's and 1940's"*

82. Family memories from Jimmy Gallippi's children.

83. *"The Italian Immigrant Experience in America"* 1970-1920; Mangione,

25; www.yale.edu/ynhti/curiculum/units/1991/3/99.03.06

84. wikipedia.org/wiki *"Redirected from U.S. economy & Business-1900-1909"*

85. wikipedia.org/wiki/ *"Immigration Act of 1906"*

86. Ibid.

87. *"Lives of Their Own, Blacks, Italians & Poles in Pittsburgh, 1900-1960"*, John Bodner, Roger Simon and Michael P. Weber.

88. *"The Italian Immigrant Experience in America"* 1970-1920; Mangione, 25; www.yale.edu/ynhti/curiculum/units/1991/3/99.03.06

89. wikipedia.org/wiki *"Pittsburgh in the 1930's and 1940's"*

90. Ibid.

91. Ibid.

92. wikipedia.org/wiki/prefrontal_lobotomy

93. en.m.wikipedia.org (Renaussance 1946-1973)

94. "Lives of Their Own, Blacks, Italians & Poles in Pittsburgh, 1900-1960", John Bodner, Roger Simon and Michael P. Weber. page 148

95. Ibid. 146

96. Ibid.

97. Ibid.

ACKNOWLEDGEMENTS

Thank you to all Gallippi and Gaetano cousins who provided pictures, information and memories. They are: Joseph Gallippi, Michael Gallippi, Bobby Gallippi, Joe Caschera, Deanna Chouinard, Linda Areyan, Nancy Schow, Ross Scarano, Emil Scarano, Emily Kelley, Ruth Gronostaj, Joe Dudash, Bernadette Gallippi, Gail Divito, Billy Gallippi, Jimmy Gallippi, Richard Gallippi, Gail Stevens, Elaine Liszewski, Sharon Coffey *(who did such a thorough job of providing family pictures along with the Gallippi family tree that was most helpful),* Karen Mayers, Tony Teti, Tina Teti, Joan Suhoza, Carol Bainbridge, Maria Kontros, Louis Gaetano, John Gaetano, Rose Papperilla, & Karen and Anthony Gaetano.

Also, I thank the following:

My sister **Janet Gebler** for providing a plethora of information, and brother-in-law **Douglas Gebler** for his valuable input.

My friend **Dan Schuckers,** who first suggested I take on this enormous task and more than encouraged me to finish it. Also for introducing me to **PA Commonwealth Court President Judge Dan Pellegrini,** who as a child, lived in the Italian Community of E. Liberty at the same time I did. I didn't know him then because he attended St. Peter and St. Paul School on Larimer Avenue while I attended Larimer Avenue School several blocks away. He has graciously shared his childhood memories and provided various important reference materials that were used in this social history. Judge Pellegrini, much like my many cousins, is an example of the applied philosophy of assimilation and success that governed our generation.

Peter M. Goda, Sr. for his inspiration, photography and for providing salient comment on the draft of this book; and **Judy and Peter Culshaw,** for their valuable assistance in editing the text of this book.

Printed in the United States
By Bookmasters